# One Good Film Deserves Another

# One Good Film Deserves Another

Michael B. Druxman

*South Brunswick and New York: A. S. Barnes and Company*
*London: Thomas Yoseloff Ltd*

A. S. Barnes and Co., Inc.
Cranbury, New Jersey 08512

Thomas Yoseloff Ltd
Magdalen House
136–148 Tooley Street
London S.W. 14, England

Library of Congress Cataloging in Publication Data

Druxman, Michael B        1941–
  One good film deserves another.

  Includes filmographies.
  1.  Moving-picture sequels.  I.  Title.
PN1995.9.S29D7        791.43′0973        76-10872
ISBN 0-498-01806-7

PRINTED IN THE UNITED STATES OF AMERICA

*For Sandra, Brian, and Cathy*

# Contents

# Acknowledgments

Grateful acknowledgment is made to the many individuals and organizations who gave of their time, their knowledge, loaned films for viewing purposes, and/or helped gather stills in preparation of this book:

Academy of Motion Picture Arts and Sciences, William Alland, Audio-Brandon Films, Edwin Blum, Bond Street Books, Eddie Brandt, Milton Bren, Jerry Bresler, Budget Films, Richard Carlson, Richard Castellano, Cherokee Books, Columbia Pictures, Philip D'Antoni, Jane Bryan Dart, Delmer Daves, Edward Dmytryk, Jose Ferrer, Films, Inc., David Foster, George Froeschel, Cary Grant, Talbot Jennings, Steve Kanaly, KCOP-TV, KHJ-TV, KTLA, KTTV, Larry Edmunds Bookshop, Henry Levin, Metro-Goldwyn-Mayer, John Milius, Sidney Miller, Walter Mirisch, John Monks, Jr., Art Murphy, Paramount Pictures, Walter Pidgeon, Robert Rosen, Arthur Ross, Herb Ross, Stanley Rubin, James Sangster, Dore Schary, George Sherman, Stirling Silliphant, Sidney Skolsky, John Sturges, J. Lee Thompson, Twentieth Century-Fox, Universal Pictures, United Artists Corporation, Hal Wallis, Warner Brothers, and Al Zimbalist.

# Preface

After completing *Make It Again, Sam,* my 1975 book about movie remakes, it seemed only natural that a complementary volume—this one dealing with film sequels—should be a future project.

Like *Sam,* the work would have an Introduction, followed by twenty-five chapters, each discussing a picture and its subsequent sequel(s). These chapters[1] would attempt, as much as possible, to answer three questions: (1) How did the sequel come to be made? (2) How were the original film's characters and story line expanded to make the follow-up? (3) What was the critical reaction to the sequel?

Whenever they were available, individuals involved with the production of these films would be consulted.

Finally, there would be a Compendium—a long, if partial, listing of pictures and their sequels.

Determining the scope of this study became the next consideration. Essentially, I wanted to deal with two kinds of *theatrical* films: those which *continued the story* of an earlier production; and movies that, simply, *repeated characters* from another film (without any plot continuity), yet were *not* a part of a *formal* or planned motion picture series.

Low-budget series such as *Tarzan, Sherlock Holmes, Boston Blackie, Andy Hardy, Dr. Kildare, Torchy Blane, Charlie Chan,* and *Blondie* have been discussed innumerable times in film books and I have no desire to reiterate that information. Should the reader, however, wish to research this genre of movie history, he would be wise to refer to James Robert Parish's definitive *The Great Movie Series* (A. S. Barnes) or *Saturday Afternoon at the Bijou* (Arlington House), an excellent work by David Zinman.

One can make a strong argument that the James Bond pictures were part of a formal series, yet I have decided to embrace them because, in a few of those entries, there was some plot continuity from the previous film. Indeed, there are several cases where I've stretched my definition of sequels slightly, in order to include marginal situations, as well as previously neglected series which encompass only a handful of films. Certainly no guideline is inviolable.

In general, for a film to be admitted for discussion (or even listed in the Compendium), it must have some *production link* (studio, star, director, etc.) with its "father" picture, since, as even the most cursory student of the cinema knows, screenplays often bear faint resemblance to the original works upon which they were based. *Literary sequels* by renowned authors like James Fenimore Cooper (*The Deerslayer, The Last of the Mohicans*) and Jules Verne (*20,000 Leagues Under the Sea, Mysterious Island*) are, therefore, not included because they were made totally independently of each other when transferred to the screen.

This provision also eliminates films like *Son of Robin Hood, Son of Dr. Jekyll, Frankenstein's Daughter, Son of Belle Starr, Return of Dr. X, Son of Monte Cristo,* and all the other cheap exploitive productions, which, by their titles, intimate they are continuations of previous successes, but, in reality, are no such animal.

As with *Make It Again, Sam,* the material has been dealt with in a way that will, hopefully, appeal more to the film "buff," rather than to the serious cinema scholar. My intent is to both amuse and inform the *light* reader of movie memorabilia, but, at the same time, give him a firm starting point should he wish to research the subject further.

The Compendium, listing films and their sequels *not* covered in the text portion of the book, is by no means complete, but has had its entries limited to

---

1. I've limited these in-depth dissertations to films of the sound era, since there was really not a strong trend toward sequelization prior to the thirties.

those sequels that, I feel, would be of greatest interest to the reader for whom the volume is intended. Information regarding new sequels that have been announced or that are currently in production is the most recent available at press time.

Naturally, a work of this sort will foster some complaints with regard to various omissions of one sort or another. Since it is conceivable that a revised and updated edition will be published in the future, any recommendations regarding its content are welcome.

# Introduction

Blessed with a hit motion picture, modern producers often decide to capitalize on their success by devising a sequel to that film. Few of these follow-ups match the artistic merit and/or box-office viability of the original, but, if the project is brought in at a reasonable budget, it has a good chance of winding up in the black.

As far back as the silent era, filmmakers realized the profit potential of encoring fictional characters or extending a story line for which audiences had previously expressed their affection. Douglas Fairbanks, prompted by the large number of dollars earned by his *The Mark of Zorro* (1920), essayed the role of that Spanish swashbuckler's offspring in *Don Q, Son of Zorro* in 1925. Then, in 1929, the performer reprised the part of D'Artagnan in *The Iron Mask*, a character he'd played previously in *The Three Musketeers* (1921). Rudolph Valentino's final screen assignment, in fact, was *The Son of the Sheik* (1926), a sequel to his immensely popular *The Sheik* (1921).

Another wordless continuation was *Beau Sabreur* (1928), which had Gary Cooper starring as Major Henri de Beaujolais, a member of the French Foreign Legion, who had been a secondary character in the 1926 classic, *Beau Geste*. In that Ronald Colman picture, the role had been played by Norman Trevor. Both movies were from Paramount and based on novels by Christopher Wren.

Undoubtedly, the most interwoven and bizarre set of sequels to ever grace the screen were those concocted by Universal, beginning in 1931. Featuring Dracula, the Frankenstein monster, the Wolf Man, and various members of their respective families, these supernatural gems served as the inspiration for later producers wishing to exploit *their* successes in the horror genre.

*Dracula*, as portrayed with a large slice of ham by Bela Lugosi, and *Frankenstein*, with Boris Karloff as the pathetic monster, both debuted on theater screens in 1931. The public's response to these terrifying films was tremendous, decreeing to the powers at Universal that follow-ups were in order. Hence, although both the monster and his creator (Colin Clive) had perished in the original production, audiences learned in the superb *Bride of Frankenstein* (1935) that each had miraculously escaped death. (As this macabre series progressed through the years, critics became fascinated with the illogical ingenuity the screenwriters utilized to devise "scientific facts" that explained how the various monsters were continually resurrected from the "absolute" destruction they'd been subjected to in the previous chapter.)

*Dracula's Daughter*, with Gloria Holden in the title role, entertained vampire fans in 1936. Unlike her evil father, whose body she cremated, this lady of the night detested her thirst for blood and consulted a psychiatrist in a futile effort to curb the affliction.

In 1939, Basil Rathbone (as "Wolf von Frankenstein") attempted to clear his father's name by resurrecting the monster (Karloff, doing the part for the third and final time) in *Son of Frankenstein*. An excellent thriller, the movie introduced Ygor, a mad shepherd (portrayed by Bela Lugosi) who controlled the monster.

Two years later, the third member of the gruesome trio made his initial appearance—*The Wolf Man* (1941), a well-done production featuring Lon Chaney, Jr., as Lawrence Talbot, the tortured soul, who, having been bitten by a werewolf, is himself cursed to become a murderous beast when the moon is full.

It was *The Ghost of Frankenstein* in 1942—with Ygor, recovered from "fatal" gunshot wounds suffered in *Son*, taking the monster (Lon Chaney, Jr.) to the second son of Frankenstein (played by Sir

*Dracula.* Edward Van Sloan and Bela Lugosi.

*Frankenstein.* Colin Clive and Boris Karloff.

*Bride of Frankenstein.* Elsa Lanchester and Boris Karloff.

*Dracula's Daughter*. Gloria Holden.

*Son of Frankenstein*. Edgar Norton, Boris
Karloff, Basil Rathbone, and Bela Lugosi.

*The Wolf Man.* Warren William, Claude Rains, and Lon Chaney, Jr.

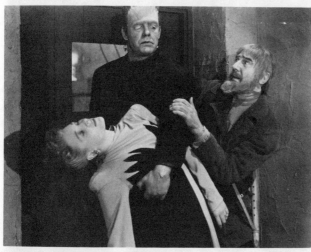

*The Ghost of Frankenstein.* Evelyn Ankers, Lon Chaney, Jr., and Bela Lugosi.

*Frankenstein Meets the Wolf Man.* Bela Lugosi and Lon Chaney, Jr.

*Son of Dracula.* Louise Allbritton and Lon Chaney, Jr.

*House of Frankenstein.* Boris Karloff and John Carradine.

*Abbott and Costello Meet Frankenstein.* Lou Costello and Lon Chaney, Jr.

*House of Dracula.* Jane Adams, Lon Chaney, Jr., Onslow Stevens, and Glenn Strange.

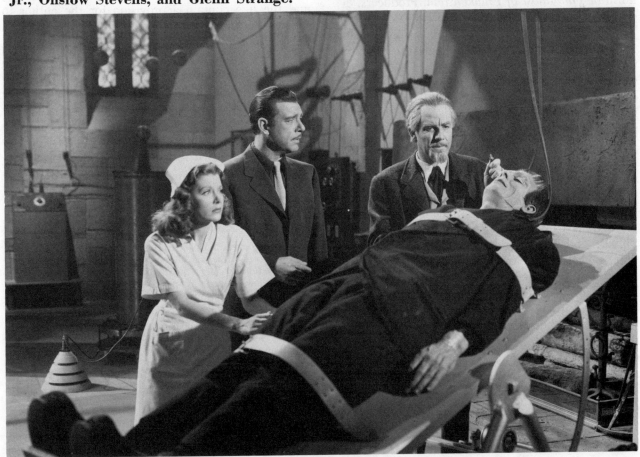

Cedric Hardwicke) for scientific help. At this entry's finish, the shepherd's evil brain has been transplanted into the monster's head, which might explain why the giant was played by Bela Lugosi in the next chapter, *Frankenstein Meets the Wolf Man* (1943). The title told all in this silly, but successful, little movie, which is notable only because it marked the first time the monsters were paired.

Also in 1943, Lon Chaney, Jr., was miscast in the title role of *Son of Dracula*, a film that had no continuity with the earlier vampire entries, but was interesting because, unlike its predecessors, it was set in the United States, rather than England or on the European continent.

The final pair of "serious" entries in this long-running series were released in 1945. Universal, trying to top themselves after *Frankenstein Meets the Wolf Man,* decided to throw a third monster into the pot and the obvious choice was Dracula. Cadaverous John Carradine played the Count in both *House of Frankenstein* and *House of Dracula,* produced on minimum budgets in an effort to squeeze out every last dollar of profit from this once imaginative group of films. Chaney, of course, was the Wolf Man, and Glenn Strange the Frankenstein monster in these pictures, which, simply, rehashed the dialogue and situations from the preceding chapters. (Viewers didn't really have to be too sharp to recognize that the climactic scene of *House of Dracula,* in which the Frankenstein monster perishes in a fire, was actually footage borrowed from the finish of *The Ghost of Frankenstein.* Producers, evidently, figured that people wouldn't notice their "fast one," or, perhaps, they simply didn't care.)

Universal's favorite monsters made their final appearances in 1948 in the hilarious *Abbott and Costello Meet Frankenstein,* a deft combination of comedy and horror, featuring Chaney and Strange in their previous roles, as well as Bela Lugosi reprising the part he had created—Dracula.

Over the years, a number of nature's and/or science's weird creatures have occupied movie screens of the world, many making subsequent appearances for as long as the public has been willing to pay their dollars to gasp at them. The Mummy (also from Universal), the Fly, Count Yorga, Dr. Phibes, and all the rest may have, in their film debuts, been unique unto themselves, however, once either they or their "sons" or "daughters" began to "return" or "rise again" to seek "revenge" or settle a "curse," then, almost without exception, the producers of these shockers, whether they realized it or not, began to borrow concepts and basic plot elements in varying degrees from the Frankenstein/

Dracula/Wolf Man films. After all, if their own pat material no longer held possibilities for continuing their narratives, wasn't it logical to look to a proven formula for "new" ideas?

The Universal "epics" may not have been unadulterated art, but they certainly created an ongoing tradition.

Horror/sci-fi follow-ups are, of course, in a category by themselves, although they do have factors in common with sequels that are less juvenile in their subject matter.

All sequels, for example, are spin-offs of previously successful films, therefore being enhanced by a presold story, characters, and, on occasion, a title.[1] Additionally, they are, usually, less expensive to produce than the original film because of their ability to reuse already completed sets, costumes, and props. An exception to this rule is the James Bond series of pictures, which, due to expensive locations and exotic special effects, has a budget that goes up and down—by millions—depending on the plot requirements of a particular episode.

Until relatively recently, sequel producers did not have to concern themselves with purchasing original story rights for their projects, since that expense, more than likely, was covered in the budget of the first picture. Truly, when the major studios controlled Hollywood production, literary material was almost always bought in perpetuity.[2] However, now, most contracts for the purchase of books, plays, and the like contain a provision for the author to receive an additional payment, should a sequel(s) be made from his work.

One writer who was denied sequel royalties in recent years was novelist John Ball, creator of black police detective Virgil Tibbs—the character portrayed by Sidney Poitier in the Academy Award-winning *In the Heat of the Night* (1967). Due to a foul-up in contract negotiations, Ball received no additional fees when Mirisch/United Artists produced two more movies—*They Call Me Mister Tibbs* (1970) and *The Organization* (1971)—starring Poitier as the homicide expert.

---

1. Distributors must make it clear to the public that their film is, in fact, a *sequel.* Robert Rosen, producer of *French Connection II,* claims the disappointing box office on his fine picture was due, in part, to the general moviegoers' ignorance that this film was a continuation, and *not* a reissue of the first film.

2. Since there were, compared to today's output, considerably fewer sequels produced in the thirties and forties, most authors felt negotiations for those rights were merely academic.

On the negative side of the coin, today's sequel producer finds it expensive, if it is even possible, to duplicate the cast he had in the original picture. Often, an actor does not want to repeat a role, feeling the assignment lacks challenge and/or that he might become type-cast. Nevertheless, if he does prove available, his agents will demand—and rightly so—a premium price for his services and, if that figure is not too far out of line, they'll, indeed, get it.[3]

In days long past, when stars were under contract to studios, there was seldom a problem in duplicating casts. This meant that, at Warner Brothers, the Lane sisters, Claude Rains, Jeffrey Lynn, and Gale Page all repeated the roles they'd created for *Four Daughters* (1938) in two spin-off pictures, *Four Wives* (1939) and *Four Mothers* (1941). Over at Metro, there was no problem in reassembling Spencer Tracy, Elizabeth Taylor, Joan Bennett, and the rest of the players from *Father of the Bride* (1950) for *Father's Little Dividend* (1951).

Few recent follow-ups have been able to reclaim

3. If the producer can't make a deal for his original actor, he'll either cast somebody else or, if possible, write the role out of the picture.

all their original players, although *Class of '44* (1973) did snag the three youthful stars—Gary Grimes, Jerry Houser, and Oliver Conant—of the nostalgic *Summer of '42* (1971) for this not-so-touching, yet entertaining, sequel. *Class* was certainly a valid continuation of its predecessor, pursuing the lads as they progressed, via different avenues, toward manhood, but its episodic structure and lack of dramatic focus denied it the poignancy

**Class of '44. Deborah Winters and Gary Grimes.**

**Summer of '42. Jerry Houser, Oliver Conant, and Gary Grimes.**

that had made *Summer* such a memorable experience.

More common is for the sequel to boast a few cast changes, if not a complete overhaul: Susan Hampshire and Nigel Davenport played the Adamsons in *Living Free* (1972), roles originally essayed by real-life husband and wife Virginia McKenna and Bill Travers in the much acclaimed saga of lions, *Born Free* (1966); Bo Svenson replaced Joe Don Baker as Sheriff Buford Pusser in *Part II, Walking Tall* (1975); and the James Bond series has featured three different actors—Sean Connery, George Lazenby, and Roger Moore—as 007.

*The Magnificent Seven* (1960) was a lusty western[4] that spawned three followups. Directed by John Sturges on Mexican locations, it starred Yul Brynner as a gunfighter named Chris, who, with six companions—Steve McQueen, Robert Vaughn, Charles Bronson, Horst Buchholz, James Coburn (replacing Sterling Hayden), and Brad Dexter—journeys to Mexico to save a village of peons from brutal bandido Eli Wallach. The Mirisch production garnered a respectable gross in this country, but made many more millions in foreign situations—assuring star status to all members of the cast, except Dexter, who later tried his hand as a film producer.

After the final shoot-out in *Seven,* only Brynner, McQueen, and Buchholz had survived and their characters were incorporated into an entertaining 1966 continuation, *Return of the Seven,* directed in Spain by Burt Kennedy. Producer Walter Mirisch: "Brynner was brought into the sequel immediately, but we never tried to get McQueen or Buchholz because, by that time, both were stars in their own right and, aside from being too expensive, would never have accepted these secondary roles."

Instead, Robert Fuller and Julien Mateos stepped in for McQueen and Buchholz respectively, and they were joined by four new recruits, including Warren Oates and Claude Akins, in a fight to free the captive peons from a psychotic Mexican land owner (Emilio Fernandez).

*Return* was also a success—especially in the foreign marketplace—prompting the Mirischs to film *Guns of the Magnificent Seven* (1969), directed in Spain by Paul Wendkos and starring George Kennedy as Chris. In this segment, the gunfighter had a whole new crew with him—James Whitmore, Joe Don Baker, Monte Markham, Bernie Casey, Reni Santoni, and Scott Thomas. Villain of the piece was Michael Ansara, commandant of an infamous military prison.

4. It was based on the Japanese film, *The Seven Samurai* (1954).

***The Magnificent Seven.* Yul Brynner and Steve McQueen.**

***Return of the Seven.* Robert Fuller and Yul Brynner.**

The film, though containing some good performances, was hampered by an uninspired script and limp direction. Yet, again, foreign countries loved it.

Walter Mirisch made no pretenses when he announced plans to produce the final episode in this western quartet—*The Magnificent Seven Ride* (1972)—to be filmed for a mere one million dollars in Southern California on a short, thirty-day shooting schedule. Lee Van Cleef, a major star of spaghetti westerns, was signed to play an aging Chris, now married and working as a lawman in a small town. After his wife is murdered, he and a new group of seven companions (including Michael Callan, Luke Askew, and Ed Lauter) help a town of widows fight off a Mexican desperado.

*Ride* was a "rip-off"[5]—an insult to its origins.

5. A sequel that adds nothing to the original plot or characters, but is made *solely* for the purpose of earning money.

*Guns of the Magnificent Seven.* **George Kennedy and Joe Don Baker.**

Routinely directed by George McCowan, the picture was cursed with a ludicrous script by Arthur Rowe, which paid no attention to facts established in the preceding productions. In one scene, for example, Chris is visited by an old friend named "Jim MacKay" (Ralph Waite) and they reminisce about the *first time* they went across the border to aid the peons. Seemingly, this character is *meant* to be a recast Steve McQueen, since he, Chris, and Buchholtz, who'd remained in Mexico to become a farmer, were the only survivors of the initial movie. That being the case, would it have been too much to ask of Rowe that he give that character the same name both McQueen and, later, Fuller had. *They* were known as "Vin."

Also out of place in the production was the reuse of Elmer Bernstein's memorable score—the theme from *The Magnificent Seven.* An asset to the earlier episodes, it seemed rather ridiculous hearing it again in such a cheap little "B" western.

*The Magnificent Seven* and its various sequels present a perfect example of how producers can ex-

*The Magnificent Seven Ride.* **Lee Van Cleef, Luke Askew, and players.**

19

ploit a once-excellent premise with negative results. Because the producing, directing, and writing talents did nothing more in their continuations than rehash the well-drawn story and characters of the original, each segment was increasingly worse than the one before it. Veritably, the films did make money outside the United States, but, at the same time, they depreciated the memory of one of the best westerns of the 1960s.

Stanley Rubin, producer of *River of No Return* and *The President's Analyst*: "If a sequel is going to be truly successful, it must explore the plot and characters of the original with more depth. Sometimes it's difficult, if not impossible, to expand on a story."

Director Herb Ross (*The Sunshine Boys, Funny Lady*) goes along with this thinking: "The main problem with sequels is one of integrity. One must be very conscious of not doing a 'rip-off.' Intentions should be serious and proper time and money spent."

"Sequels should have a creative, as well as a financial, motive," says screenwriter/producer Stirling Silliphant (*In the Heat of the Night, Charly*). "Many movies don't lend themselves toward sequelization, but those that do should be studied carefully by the makers of the follow-up, so they can spot and evaluate the mistakes, thereby coming up with a better picture."

At this writing, Silliphant was working on the script for the third movie about "Harry Callahan," the unorthodox San Francisco cop played by Clint Eastwood in *Dirty Harry* (1971) and *Magnum Force* (1973). Productions of this nature might best be termed "character sequels," since they allow an established star to repeat a role he (and the public) particularly enjoys, without commiting himself to a *formal* series. These spin-offs do not extend the story line of the earlier film and, in a sense, are merely "the further adventures of" that particular character.

After winning an Academy Award for his portrayal of Father Chuck O'Malley in *Going My Way* (1944), Bing Crosby chose to essay that part a second time in *The Bells of St. Mary's* (1945), in which he co-starred with Ingrid Bergman; and John Wayne, garnering his Oscar for his Wallace Beery-like marshal in *True Grit* (1969), jumped at the opportunity to do the role again in *Rooster Cogburn* (1975), a production that, for the first time, paired him with Katharine Hepburn. Despite the generous budgets and technical expertise with which both these sequels were produced, neither truly succeeded in furthering the development of their respective established characters. The final result was two pleasant, but certainly less than memorable, entertainments.

Conversely, except for a far-fetched ending, *Magnum Force* was a prime example of what a character sequel *should* be, in that it stuck Harry Callahan into a situation that required him to utilize an entirely different set of values from those he'd relied on his first time out. Tautly directed by Don Siegel, *Dirty Harry* was a brutal, well-constructed thriller, which had Eastwood as Callahan far overstepping the letter of the law in his efforts to capture a dangerous killer. *Magnum*, on the other hand, pitted the violent cop against a police "death squad," necessitating him to argue against one's taking the law into his own hands.

John Milius, who, with Mike Cimino, scripted *Magnum Force*, discusses the two projects: "In *Harry*, we argued that it is sometimes necessary to go beyond the law, then, in the second film, we answered that proposition by saying it's not that simple. There are bad implications when you set yourself above the rules—no matter how just your cause.

"I really like Harry," continues Milius. "He's to the seventies what Bond was to the sixties. The

***Dirty Harry.* Clint Eastwood.**

audiences love his methods and identify with him. Take the plane hijacking sequence in *Magnum Force,* for example. It's a terribly frustrating situation that Harry solves in his primitive fashion—he kills the 'bad guys.'"

Milius, who worked on the screenplay for *Dirty Harry* also, but did not receive credit, dislikes doing sequels: "For me, they're a 'pain in the ass,' because they're *too* easy. If you did the first script, then you've been there before."

The initial two Harry Callahan entries were, indeed, intelligent, above average action pictures. Hopefully, future episodes will continue that tradition.

*The Lion in Winter* (1968) was another type of character sequel. In this superb filmization of James Goldman's fiery play, Peter O'Toole played an older version of Henry II, a role he'd first essayed in *Becket* (1964). Though the actor was the only connecting link between these two fine films, which were produced by different companies, his sensitive expanded study of the tortured monarch unified the pictures into a single entity. Incidentally, Henry's wife, Eleanor of Aquitaine, a minor role played by Pamela Brown in *Becket,* shared the screen equally when done by Katharine Hepburn in *Lion.*

An unusual pair of sequels were those dealing with the life of Thomas A. Edison, filmed concurrently by MGM for release in 1940. Dore Schary, one of the writers on the films, recalls how they came about: "John Considine, the producer, originally wanted to do one long picture honoring Edison. Mickey Rooney would play the boy, then we'd *dissolve* and Spencer Tracy would be the adult. It didn't take us long to realize that such an optical effect would produce the biggest laugh in the history of movies, so we decided to divide the project in half."

*Young Tom Edison,* starring Rooney, was on theater screens in February and the superior Tracy contribution, *Edison, the Man,* appeared in May— probably the shortest time to ever elapse between the release of an original film and its follow-up. Of course, it isn't often that two such related pictures are conceived and shot at the same time either.

Sequels, more often than not, will develop the previous picture's plot line in a forward direction. *The Return of Frank James* (1940) starred Henry Fonda as the notorious outlaw, who spends the entire film chasing the killers of his brother, shot to death in *Jesse James* (1939). The original picture, with Tyrone Power in the title role, contained several fictional elements, but there was no truth in the continuation whatsoever. Both films, nevertheless, entertained audiences and remain minor classics of the genre.

More recently, producer Ray Stark acquired the rights to the Humphrey Bogart classic, *The Maltese*

*Magnum Force.* **Hal Holbrook and Clint Eastwood.**

*Becket.* Martita Hunt, Peter O'Toole, and Pamela Brown.

*The Lion in Winter.* Peter O'Toole and Katharine Hepburn.

*Falcon,* and made a deal to produce a sequel for Columbia. George Segal was Sam Spade, *Jr.,* and he was joined by Lee Patrick and Elisha Cook, Jr., reprising their roles from the 1941 original. Played as a comedy, *The Black Bird* (1975) had the reluctant private-eye being approached by an assortment of unusual characters—all of whom wanted the Falcon, which, thirty-four years before, Sydney Greenstreet led us to believe was a fake.

Spin-offs that serve as prologues to their original pictures are interesting challenges for filmmakers, in that the writers must make assumptions as to how the already established characters developed into what they were in the first movie. A perfect example is *The Nightcomers* (1972) starring Marlon Brando, a little-known picture by Michael Winner, which theorized as to how the children in Henry James's immortal *The Turn of the Screw* came to be possessed by the ghosts of Peter Quint and Miss Jessel. That novel had been filmed in 1962 as *The Innocents,* with Deborah Kerr, and, from a production standpoint, bore no relationship to Winner's plodding melodrama.

False sequels are those pictures which bear only

**_Son of Captain Blood._ Sean Flynn**

a faint plot and character relationship to the films upon which they claim to be based, but employ a familiar title to, hopefully, ensure a reasonable box-office response. Aside from George Kennedy's repeating his previous role, there was absolutely no story connection between *Airport* (1970) and 1974's *Airport 1975*. (But, really, if one wants to make another airline disaster picture, is there a better tag for it?)

The Italian-made *Son of Captain Blood* (1962) had even less validity as a sequel, since, production-wise, no link existed between it and the classic 1935 Errol Flynn swashbuckler, *Captain Blood*. Wisely, the producers of this inept actioner decided to cast Sean Flynn, the son of the late star, in the title role, thereby generating a certain curiosity value and, also, giving its status as a follow-up the slightest of justifications.

In the case of *Return to Macon County* (1975), producers completely ignored the surviving characters and plot of their runaway success, *Macon County Line* (1974), and, instead, devised an entirely new story that contained many of the elements that were inherent in the first film.

As this is being written, a number of sequels are in various stages of preproduction. Among the successful films serving as the basis for these spin-offs are: *The Sting, Earthquake, The Poseidon Adventure, Death Race 2000, Chinatown, Jaws,* and even *Gone With The Wind.*

Indeed, when Steven Spielberg, director of that shark horror film, learned of Universal's plan to produce a follow-up to his picture, he announced to

*Daily Variety:* "Making a sequel to any film is just a cheap carny trick. Doing a sequel is really like operating a slot machine knowing you're going to get three cherries every time. It reduces movie-making as an art to just a science. I have seen only a couple of sequels that were as good or better than the original. *Godfather II* was one of these. It was rare, a personal statement film that was done by Coppola with love and respect—and came up with three cherries, too."

The director may have a valid argument. Over the years, many studios, in the interest of grabbing a "quick buck," have certainly ordered their sequels turned out as rapidly and inexpensively as possible—regardless of their artistic worth. Yet, by acknowledging Francis Ford Coppola's film, Spielberg admits that, when produced with care, a sequel does not necessarily have to be a "rip-off," but, in some instances, can become a masterpiece unto itself.

*Captain Blood.* **Errol Flynn.**

# 1 Boys Town

"There is no such thing as a bad boy."

This was the philosophy of Father Edward J. Flanagan, who, in 1917, borrowed ninety dollars from a Jewish pawnbroker for rent on a house (in Omaha, Nebraska), which was to provide a proper environment for neglected, homeless, and wayward boys. By giving these youths the best possible training and surroundings, the Roman Catholic priest believed that his charges would not choose a nefarious life, but would enter the adult world as substantial citizens.

It wasn't long before Father Flanagan and his boys had outgrown that first house, and were forced to find more space. Through donations by concerned citizens, the priest purchased the 320-acre Overlook Farm, located on the Lincoln Highway near Omaha. Classrooms, dormitories, and other facilities were constructed—the project ultimately increasing in size to one thousand acres. Soon, Overlook Farms was rechristened "Boys Town," incorporated in 1936.

John W. Considine, Jr., a producer at MGM, heard of Boys Town and realized that the story of Father Flanagan's crusade could provide the basis for a good, albeit modestly budgeted, family motion picture. With the approval of studio boss Louis B. Mayer, a story line was developed—the idea being that Spencer Tracy would play the institution's founder, supported by Freddie Bartholomew and up-and-coming Mickey Rooney as two of the unfortunate lads.

Writer Dore Schary, who, in later years, was to run MGM, recalls the afternoon Considine summoned him to his office to discuss the proposed film: "I'd never heard of Boys Town, but, since I'd worked as a counselor in boys' camps, I was immediately interested in the project.

"Considine wasn't happy with the plot he had, but wasn't sure how it could be fixed. I looked it over and suggested that the well-bred Freddie Bartholomew character was completely wrong for the story. Considine agreed. The part was dropped, a script written, and, from that point, everything seemed to work."

Initially, Spencer Tracy refused to play the role of Flanagan. Aside from his feelings that it would be difficult to accurately transfer the qualities of this warm and dedicated human being to celluloid, the actor didn't really want to enact another priest, since he'd recently essayed a cleric in *San Francisco* (1936). However, since that was the best assignment the studio was offering him at the moment, he acquiesced.

To avoid the costly problems of aging characters and duplicating Boys Town during its formative years, the screenplay by Dore Schary and John Meehan (from a story by Mr. Schary and Eleanore Griffin) began its action during the first years of the Depression, rather than 1917.

We first see Flanagan (Tracy) visiting an about-to-be executed death row convict (Leslie Fenton), who tells the priest that if he'd had one friend as a boy, he would not have followed a criminal career. Moved by this admission, Flanagan decides to set up a home for unwanted boys, borrowing some money from pawnbroker friend Dave Morris (Henry Hull) to rent an old house. Chances for the project's survival are bleak at first, but, thanks to donations, the current site of the institution is purchased and permanent buildings constructed. Yet, financial problems continue to plague Boys Town.

Whitey Marsh (Rooney), a tough punk-kid with a hoodlum brother (Edward Norris), comes to the now-sprawling institution, causing nothing but trouble with the other youths. His attitude changes, however, when he inadvertently is responsible for young Pee Wee (Bobs Watson) being hit by a car. The child, who hero-worships the older lad, survives, and Whitey becomes a respectable citizen at Boys Town, later aiding Flanagan in the capture of his gangster brother, Joe.

At the film's conclusion, Father Flanagan announces, to Morris's dismay (since the pawnbroker will have to find the funding), that he is going to expand Boys Town to accommodate many more youngsters.

*Boys Town* (1938) was shot, in part, at the Omaha school, under the fast-paced direction of Norman Taurog, the foremost director of young actors in Hollywood.

Metro executives were certainly surprised when the film turned into a box-office hit. Most had considered the project to be an above-average *program* picture. Nevertheless, both the public and critics alike took to this sensitive, entertaining story and, for the most part, "forgave" its creators for marring the production with some overly melodramatic sequences (the incidents involving Whitey's brother) near its conclusion.

The *New York Times:* "It manages, in spite of the embarrassing sentimentality of its closing scenes, to be a consistently interesting and frequently touching motion picture. . . . Spencer Tracy's performance of Father Flanagan—like Spencer Tracy's performances of almost anyone—is perfection itself and the most eloquent tribute to the Nebraska priest."

Tracy won an Oscar for his participation in this production (he'd also received the same award a year earlier for *Captains Courageous*), as did Mr. Schary and Miss Griffin for their original story. Most gratifying, the picture called America's attention to the institution known as Boys Town and, as a result, that worthy venture received several million dollars in donations.

*Boys Town.* **Spencer Tracy and Mickey Rooney.**

*Boys Town.* **Spencer Tracy, Henry Hull, and players.**

"The public 'demanded' a sequel to *Boys Town*," recalls Sidney Miller, who had played Mo Kahn, one of the school's young leaders. "Metro received letters from all over the country, asking them to do another movie about Father Flanagan."

Not wishing to disappoint the ticket-buyers, John Considine set writer James Kevin McGuinness to fashion a follow-up story and screenplay to the popular 1938 production. Again, Norman Taurog was set to direct, but to save money, location filming was nixed in favor of building the Boys Town exteriors on the huge MGM backlot. After some

hesitation, Tracy agreed to reprise his Oscar-winning role, and, also returning were Masters Rooney, Miller, and Watson. Henry Hull was unavailable when the movie went into production, so Dave Morris was portrayed by Lee J. Cobb.

*Men of Boys Town* (1941) was little more than a rehash of its predecessor's basic material. Father Flanagan continues his fight to help unfortunate boys, while trying to keep his school financially solvent—a battle he almost loses this time out. He also has a crippled and embittered youth on his hands, but the lad (Larry Nunn) is shocked into walking when his pet dog is killed by a truck. (Certainly this was reminiscent of Whitey's rapid conversion after Pee Wee's accident in *Boys Town*.)

Whitey is adopted by the Maitlands (Henry O'Neill and Mary Nash), a wealthy older couple; helps a youngster (Darryl Hickman) escape from a harsh and corrupt reformatory; and, when his complicity is discovered, is sent to that same state institution himself. Father Flanagan, of course, comes to the boy's rescue, exposing the reformatory officials' evil ways.

**Boys Town. Frank Thomas, Spencer Tracy, Mickey Rooney, Sidney Miller, and players.**

**Boys Town. Spencer Tracy and Leslie Fenton.**

*Men of Boys Town.* Addison Richards, Henry O'Neill, Mary Nash, Mickey Rooney, Spencer Tracy, and Darryl Hickman.

*Men of Boys Town.* Henry O'Neill, Mickey Rooney, Lee J. Cobb, and Mary Nash.

*Men of Boys Town.* Ben Welden and Spencer Tracy.

Disillusioned with the rich life he'd been living with his stepparents, Whitey decides to return to Boys Town and Mr. Maitland agrees to furnish the capital needed to save the school.

Though performances in *Men of Boys Town* equaled those of the earlier movie, Mr. McGuinness's uninspired screenplay did not. The contrived story line offered situations that were far too pat (like Whitey's being sent to the same reformatory where young Nunn had been hurt), and, in a couple of instances, stopped the forward progress of the plot altogether to allow Mickey Rooney an opportunity to perform some unfunny comedy sketches.

The *New York Times* referred to the effort as ". . . an obvious and maudlin reassembly of cliches out of the cabinet marked Pathos, lacking completely the sincerity which did distinguish the first, and so frequently punctuated by close-ups of blubbering boys that one finally feels an embarrassed inclination to look away. A noble and worthy institution is certainly not enhanced by this film."

Regardless of remarks like these, *Men of Boys Town* did extremely well financially, though grosses did not equal those of the parent feature.

Father Edward J. Flanagan died in 1948—at a time when the institution he founded boasted a population of nine hundred boys. Today, his fine work continues, carried on by those who succeed him.

*Boys Town* and *Men of Boys Town* may have filled the coffers at Metro-Goldwyn-Mayer, but, by enlisting the interest of many wealthy benefactors, they also ensured the survival of Father Flanagan's dream to turn needy boys into outstanding men.

## FILMOGRAPHY

1938: *Boys Town* (MGM/Norman Taurog) Spencer Tracy.

1941: *Men of Boys Town* (MGM/Norman Taurog) Spencer Tracy.

# 2 *Topper*

The idea of having characters vanish, then reappear again, on the motion picture screen was nothing new in 1937. This piece of camera trickery had been employed—with varying degrees of accomplishment —since the silent era. Techniques had, naturally, improved over the years, producing such memorable experiences as James Whale's *The Invisible Man* (1933) and, from Great Britain, René Clair's *The Ghost Goes West* (1936), but Hal Roach's production of *Topper*, based on the late Thorne Smith's whimsical 1926 novel, was the first important American film to successfully utilize the effect in a strictly humorous vein. A tremendous hit with the public, the 1937 release was an unique blend of slapstick, sophistication, and the supernatural, and, though flawed, ultimately began a new trend in movie comedy.

Cary Grant, unhappy with his contract at Paramount,[1] decided to free-lance after his deal with the major studio expired. One of the first offers he accepted as an independent was from producer Roach, who had been planning to do the Thorne Smith comedy for some time. Recalls the actor: "I loved the story so much that I agreed to help Roach with the financing of the picture by deferring my salary until he'd made a deal for distribution. Up until then, I would be reimbursed for my expenses only."[2]

Grant was to play rich, whacky George Kerby, who, with his equally screwball wife, Marion, is killed in an automobile accident. Unable to get into heaven until they perform a good deed, the Kerby's decide that they will revitalize the dull life of their friend, banker Cosmo Topper, married to a scatter-brained wife.

Often invisible or transparent, George and Marion are successful in their mission, introducing Cosmo to their fast, champagne-sparkling former existence. Along the way, Topper becomes involved in a street brawl and has many problems trying to explain to bewildered humans why inanimate objects are moving through the air about him. Yet, at film's end, the milquetoast has changed in personality to a man-about-town.

Initially discussed as co-stars for Grant were Jean Harlow as Marion and W. C. Fields in the title role, but these players' respective studios (MGM and Paramount) were not about to loan their valuable properties out to Hal Roach without a hefty fee in exchange, which, of course, the independent producer could not afford. Instead, Roland Young was signed to play Topper and Constance Bennett, the vivacious Marion.

"Connie's career had slipped a bit the past few years," reflects Mr. Grant, "so she wasn't as expensive to get as Harlow. Nevertheless, she started to make demands immediately—the first one being that I be replaced by Fred MacMurray. Hal explained to her that that was impossible, but to placate her, I allowed her to have top billing."

Billie Burke was hired to play Mrs. Topper and Alan Mowbray signed on as Wilkins, the very

---

1. He felt he was only getting assigned to the "leftover" roles fellow contractees like Gary Cooper had already refused.
2. Halfway through principal photography, a financing/distribution deal was made with MGM and Grant was paid his full salary.

*Topper*. Roland Young, Cary Grant, and Constance Bennett.

*Topper*. Billie Burke, Alan Mowbray, and Cary Grant.

proper family butler. The latter part of the screenplay, authored by Jack Jevne, Eric Hatch, and Eddie Moran, had Cosmo and Marion going to the Sea Breeze Hotel together and sharing a room. This delicate situation, in which the hotel employees suspect that Topper has a woman in his room for immoral purposes (they'd heard voices), only to learn upon searching the premises that he is "alone," allowed for the introduction of two scene-stealing characters —a house detective (Eugene Pallette) and the elevator boy (Arthur Lake).

Though audiences were delighted with the special photographic effects by Roy Seawright, most critics were less than thrilled about the film as a whole. *Variety:* "Effort to excuse the story's absurdities on the theory that the intent is farce comedy does not entirely excuse the production from severe rebuke.

Fact also that the living dead always are facetious may be shocking to sensibilities. Some of the situations and dialogue offend conventional good taste."

In fact, the writers had concocted a rather plodding screenplay for a comedy and the equally heavy-handed direction by Norman Z. McLeod didn't help matters. By today's standards, the film is rather dull, and one can only assume that the novelty of disappearing ghosts and autos driving by themselves, as well as the actors' deft performances—still a joy to watch—were responsible for the enthusiastic reaction by 1937 moviegoers. It was this picture and his subsequent *The Awful Truth* that started Cary Grant on the way to becoming the screen's most popular performer of sophisticated light comedy. Roland Young also fared well, garnering a supporting actor Oscar nomination for his portrayal, and Constance Bennett's career received a needed boost.

With *Topper* such a commercial success, it wasn't long before Roach decided to film Thorne Smith's sequel, *Topper Takes a Trip*. Milton H. Bren, associate producer on the initial picture, was given the full title this time and immediately found himself with a major casting problem. Bren: "Constance Bennett, in violation of an option she'd given us when she did the first film, had signed to do another project, which conflicted with the sequel's start date and caused it to be delayed for two months. Cary Grant, on the other hand, was not available when Connie was free, so we decided, rather than delay the picture any longer, to go ahead without Cary, since the story could work without George, but *not* without Marion.

"Cary graciously allowed us to use scenes from *Topper* in this film in order to re-establish the basic situation."

Roland Young, Billie Burke, and Alan Mowbray repeated their previous assignments for this United Artists release, as did Norman Z. McLeod as director. Screenplay credit was shared by Eddie Moran, Jack Jevne, and Corey Ford. Roy Seabright again handled special photographic effects, improving upon what he'd created in 1937.

As the picture begins, Marion is alone—George having accomplished *his* good deed and departed for heaven. The late Mrs. Kerby, with the aid of a ghostly wire terrier named Mr. Atlas (Skippy), decides to again help Cosmo, who is being sued by his wife for divorce. Mrs. Topper is angry at her husband because of his reported escapade at the Sea Breeze Hotel (from the first picture) and, upon the advice of her "friend," Mrs. Parkhurst (Verree

Teasdale), has filed this civil action, which the judge denies.

The often-divorced Mrs. Parkhurst convinces Mrs. Topper that she should go to the French Riviera to obtain her freedom. Cosmo, Marion, and Mr. Atlas follow in short order and learn that the giddy woman has been delivered by her advisor into the hands of fortune hunter Baron de Rossi (Alexander D'Arcy) and his associate, Louis (Franklin Pangborn). Naturally, Topper eventually wins back his wife and, as the reunited couple fly back to the United States, we see that Marion will now be reunited with George.

*Topper Takes a Trip* (1939) was a vast improvement over its predecessor. This time, the writers had skillfully constructed a diverting piece of light fluff, laced with clever lines and hilarious situations, then turned it over to McLeod, whose smart direction molded the fanciful project into one of the funniest pictures of the year. Few who saw the production can forget classic scenes like Topper's winning streak (with the aid of an invisible Marion) at the roulette table or the ectoplasmic lady's encounter with the phony baron on the beach. Buried in sand, de Rossi is quite taken aback when unseen hands remove his bathing trunks.

The best moments sprang from Topper's "impro-vised" explanations to mortals of his strange behavior. In one such scene, he is walking down a hotel hallway, chatting with the invisible Marion. Noting that a woman is watching him, he offers: "I was talking to someone else. You see, I thought I was someone else I knew . . . but I wasn't."

***Topper Takes a Trip*. Roland Young and Paul Hurst.**

***Topper Takes a Trip*. George Davis, Roland Young, Constance Bennett, and players.**

Critical reaction to the United Artists release was only luke-warm. The *New York Times:* "But the law of diminishing laughs is applying itself and eventually you are silently echoing poor Topper's appeals to be left alone to work out his own reconciliation with Mrs. Topper, who has come to Paris to get a divorce. There is, after all, such a thing as excess of spirits, even when they are embodied (and disembodied) in Constance Bennett and Skippy."

*Topper Returns,* the third and final segment in the film series, was from an original screenplay by Jonathan Latimer and Gordon Douglas. Released by United Artists in 1941, the Roach production again offered Roland Young and Billie Burke as the Toppers, but, in this instance, they were supported by an entirely new cast, under the direction of Roy Del Ruth.

Set in a mysterious old seacliff house—complete with secret passages—the story tells of Gail Richards (Joan Blondell), murdered by a hooded figure who has mistaken her for heiress Ann Carrington (Carole Landis). The buxom Miss Richards, in shadowy form, appeals to Topper for help in capturing the killer and saving the life of the intended victim. Unfortunately, Gail's body has disappeared and, when it is found, Topper is himself the chief murder suspect. But, with the spirit's help, the banker unmasks the real culprit (H. B. Warner), who is killed in his attempted escape.

The problem with this picture was that the writers never really decided if the screenplay should be a comedy/fantasy in the same vein as the previous *Topper* outings, or a straight, though humorous, whodunit. As it turned out, the latter approach seemed to prevail, which made Miss Blondell's appearances/disappearances (again courtesy of Mr. Seawright) almost superfluous. True, Del Ruth's direction kept things moving at a lively clip, but the final result was no better than some of the "B" screwball detective movies that were so prevalent during that era.

Performances were generally amusing, although Mr. Young did seem to be a trifle bored with this repetition of his role. Eddie (Rochester) Anderson, as the Topper's frightened chauffeur, supplied some of the movie's funniest moments. Wide-eyed at the ghostly happenings about him and regularly being tossed down a deep shaft into an underground grotto (where he is bullied by a seal), the accomplished comedian comments: "I'm going back to Mr. Benny. Nothing like this happens there."[3]

The *New York Times:* "But for all their efforts, they can't conceal that *Topper Returns* is old stuff. All of which indicates that one may raise a ghost, but hardly the ghost of a ghost."

The early fifties found Leo G. Carroll essaying the role of Topper in a successful television series of the same name, which featured Robert Sterling and Anne Jeffreys as the Kerbys.

The special photography and accompanying "unearthly" humor that made the initial *Topper* films such crowd-pleasers during the late thirties has been employed in innumerable—and much more effective—films in the years since the Kerbys first crashed their car into that tree. Indeed, television series like *Bewitched* and *I Dream of Jeannie*—despite their comparatively bland characterizations—may have done the same gags a lot better, but none can deny that these popular shows certainly owed their genesis to Mr. Roach and Thorne Smith.

## FILMOGRAPHY

1937: *Topper* (MGM/Norman Z. McLeod) Roland Young.
1939: *Topper Takes a Trip* (UA/Norman Z. McLeod) Roland Young.
1941: *Topper Returns* (UA/Roy Del Ruth) Roland Young.

3. Anderson was, of course, at that time a regular on the Jack Benny radio program.

*Topper Returns.* **Roland Young and Joan Blondell.**

*Topper Returns.* **Billie Burke, Patsy Kelly, and Eddie "Rochester" Anderson.**

# 3 *Brother Rat*

Though many college students write plays, few of these amateur efforts have ever been produced on the Broadway stage, and only a small percentage of these finished out a full season. Ergo, the chances of a classroom-originated project going on to become a *runaway* hit are, obviously, very slim.

John Monks, Jr., and Fred F. Finklehoffe were two young dramatists who beat the odds. As cadets together at the Virginia Military Institute, they decided to co-author a play—based on their experiences at that "West Point of the South"—for their English thesis. The result was a comedy entitled *Brother Rat*[1] and, as Monks recalls: "It was pretty bad . . . but it got us our grade."

Following graduation, the men parted ways. Finklehoffe attended Yale Law School and Monks tried his luck at becoming a professional actor. A few years passed. The aspiring attorney was waiting to take his bar exam when his former classmate approached him with the suggestion that they revise their play, then go after a Broadway production. Having nothing better to do, Finklehoffe agreed and the writers set to work.

Monks: "Thirty-two producers turned it down before George Abbott decided to take a chance on us. The production was a smash. It played 2½ years in New York and resulted in two road companies."

The original 1936 cast for *Brother Rat* included Frank Albertson, Jose Ferrer, and Eddie Albert, who, when the zany entertainment was purchased by Warner Brothers, was signed to repeat his stage role of the expectant father. According to Monks: "Fred and I didn't do the screenplay because, by that time, our price was too high." Instead, that assignment was capably handled by Richard Macaulay and Jerry Wald.

1. The friendly nickname students at that military college call each other.

Directed by William Keighley, the film was released late in 1938 and followed the New York production rather closely: Billy Randolph (Wayne Morris), Bing Edwards (Albert), and Dan Crawford (Ronald Reagan) are three first classmen at the Virginia Military Institute who involve themselves in a series of escapades that threaten their receiving final diplomas. Randolph, the "devil-may-care" cadet, and Crawford, his more practical buddy, slip out of the dormitory one night to romance Joyce Winfree (Priscilla Lane) and Claire Adams (Jane Wyman) respectively. They are caught by Miss Adams's father, Colonel Ramm (Henry O'Neill), commandant of the college, and, as punishment, he pulls them out of the school's championship baseball game.

Meanwhile, easy-going Bing, who is secretly married to Kate Rice (Jane Bryan), learns that his wife is pregnant. His two friends, apprised of the delicate situation, agree to keep this confidence so the father-to-be will not be expelled from the institution. Events move quickly now—through a series of involved situations for the trio, including a sequence where Joyce and Claire are smuggled into the boy's room to help Bing study for his chemistry final.

*Brother Rat.* **Priscilla Lane and Wayne Morris.**

*Brother Rat.* **Ronald Reagan, Wayne Morris, and Eddie Albert.**

The conclusion is a happy one, with the cadets receiving their diplomas from Colonel Ramm, who gets a cigar in return from proud papa Bing.

*Brother Rat* was a wonderful, zany, accelerated comedy that featured some adept performances from six of Warners' second-string contractees. Wayne Morris was surprisingly good as the fast-talking Randolph, a fine departure from the naive country boys he'd played in films like *Kid Galahad* (1937), and the Misses Lane and Wyman were cute and saucy as the eligible young ladies. Albert, of course, making his film debut,[2] had the meatiest role and took full advantage of each and every line.

The *New York Times:* "It's an excellent transcription of the play, loyal to all its screenable material and matching the playwright's lively humors in the added scenes."

2. Signed to a term contract by the studio, Albert found himself playing a string of "slow" types like Bing Edwards. It was a number of years before Hollywood gave him the opportunity to prove himself a versatile actor.

Shortly after the movie had premiered, Monks and Finklehoffe, who were between assignments, came up with the idea of writing a sequel to their earlier hit. Monks reflects: "We wanted to progress the characters . . . to see what happened to them after they left school. So, we had our agent inquire if Warners would be interested in such a project. They were, and we sold it to them from a thirty-page outline."

*Brother Rat and a Baby* was scripted by Monks and Finklehoffe, with direction by Ray Enright. All of the principals from the first picture repeated their assignments, with the exception of Henry O'Neill, who was replaced by Moroni Olsen. For some unknown reason, this character, a colonel in the initial film, was reduced to the rank of major for the sequel and had his last name changed to "Terry."

Unfortunately, the 1940 release was a feeble follow-up to its predecessor. The story has Bing quitting his school coaching job at Metropolis, Kentucky, and journeying to New York with wife, Kate, and son, Commencement, in order to compete for the head coaching job at his alma mater. Billy, who, along with Dan, now works for his father's publishing firm, had summoned his former classmate to Gotham so that he could campaign better for the athletic position. As usual, his schemes backfire, causing Bing to lose the appointment and both he and Dan to be fired from their respective jobs. To climax his unorthodox activities, he gives a cab driver Kate's uncle's invaluable Stradivarius violin as security for an eighty-five cent fare, then is indirectly responsible (he gave Commencement a lighter to play with) for the gutting by fire of the relative's uninsured (Bing had forgotten to mail the premium check) penthouse apartment.

Billy later saves the day when he smuggles Commencement aboard a diplomatic plane bound for South America and, as a consequence, the baby becomes an international celebrity. The uncle (Berton Churchill) gives the three lads good jobs; Billy weds Joyce; Dan marries Claire; and all ends well.

Despite the uninspired script and direction, which resulted in a screen full of rapid lines and quick action, but, sadly, few laughs, the cast, for the most part (Reagan, as in the first film, was a bit stiff), acquitted themselves rather well. Nevertheless, reviews were not good. Said the *New York Times:* "*Brother Rat and a Baby* . . . continues a line of cadetish humor which was fully concluded, not to say exhausted, in the parent production; it has no plot-excuse for such an exhumation, only a series of desperate and uninspired improvisation, and, finally, it demonstrates how horrible dormitory fun can be when carried over, inexcusably, into an adult world."

Warners attempted to remake *Brother Rat* as a musical in 1952, calling their dull little Technicolor production *About Face.* Gordon MacRae, Eddie Bracken, and Dick Wesson were competent as the cadets, but the film was a pale imitation of the 1938 original, which, unlike many comedies of the thirties and forties, has remained, over the years, a very entertaining picture.

## FILMOGRAPHY

1938: *Brother Rat* (WB/William Keighley) Wayne Morris.
1940: *Brother Rat and a Baby* (WB/Ray Enright) Wayne Morris.

*Brother Rat and a Baby.* Eddie Albert, Jane Bryan, and Wayne Morris.

*Brother Rat and a Baby.* Ronald Reagan and Jane Wyman.

# 4 *The Little Foxes*

If one were asked to name the most ruthless family in dramatic literature, certainly the Hubbard clan, created by playwright Lillian Hellman in *The Little Foxes*, would merit prime consideration. Making their initial appearance on the Broadway stage in 1939, this wicked brood held no loyalty for one another and, indeed, seemed to destroy everything they touched. For Miss Hellman, the Hubbards, who came to power in the late nineteenth century through unsavory business practices, represented everything negative about the rise of industrialism in the South. They were, as the Bible said, ". . . the little foxes that spoil the vines, for our vines have tender grapes."

In New York, Tallulah Bankhead had essayed the play's pivotal character of Regina Hubbard Giddens, but when producer Samuel Goldwyn acquired the property for the screen, it was decided that a top *movie* actress—Bette Davis— should assume this role of a "black widow spider" in human form. The screenplay was by Miss Hellman, with added scenes and dialogue by Arthur Kober, Dorothy Parker, and Alan Campbell. William Wyler directed a cast that included Charles Dingle, Dan Duryea, Patricia Collinge, Carl Benton Reid, and John Marriott—all of whom were from the original Broadway cast.

The story dealt with an interfamily conspiracy to divide shares in the purchase of a cotton mill that a northern financier is bringing to the South. Regina attempts to persuade her invalid banker husband, Horace Giddens (Herbert Marshall), to put his money into the venture, so that she can have the controlling interest over her brothers, Ben (Dingle) and Oscar (Reid). Quite aware that his wife despises his benevolent ways and that the only one who truly cares for him is their lovely daughter, Alexandra (Teresa Wright), Horace refuses to agree to this unethical enterprise, which will employ cheap southern labor. Meanwhile, Leo (Duryea), son of

Oscar and his abused, balmy wife, Birdie (Miss Collinge), has, at his father's urging, stolen bonds belonging to the banker, thereby eliminating the need for a *direct* investment from him.

Events move rapidly toward a climax after Horace is stricken with a heart attack. To prevent his further interfering with her devious schemes, the viper-like Regina lets her husband die rather than get his emergency medicine. In a final confrontation with her brothers, she makes it known that she is aware of Leo's theft and, if she is to remain silent, a "new economics" will be formed: Regina will now own the lion's share (seventy-five percent) of stock in the mill. Forced to acquiesce, Ben does so "good-naturedly," while he ponders Horace's sudden death: "What is a man in a wheelchair doing on a staircase?"

Alexandra, no longer able to tolerate her mother, flees the abhorrent household, joining her writer-suitor, David Hewitt (Richard Carlson).

The 1941 RKO release was an exceptional production—one that Howard Barnes in the *New York Herald-Tribune* called "Flawless and fascinating. . . . When a really fine film comes along it is up to all of us who really like fine films to cheer. Cheer, then, this Sabbath for *The Little Foxes*. For this adaptation of a striking play is not only a great show and an absorbing entertainment, it charts a whole new course of motion picture making. . . . Bette Davis matches Miss Bankhead's splendid portrayal in the play."

Consistently during production, Miss Davis had "battled" with director Wyler over how her role should be played. She had seen *Foxes* performed in New York and felt that her predecessor in the part had presented the character in its only *proper* interpretation—that of a cold villainess. Wyler, on the other hand, argued unsuccessfully for a softer portrayal. At one point, tensions between star and

*The Little Foxes.* Herbert Marshall, Bette
Davis, Charles Dingle, and Carl Benton Reid.

*The Little Foxes.* Richard Carlson, Jessie
Grayson, and Teresa Wright.

*The Little Foxes.* Charles Dingle, Patricia Collinge, Bette Davis, Herbert Marshall, and Carl Benton Reid.

director became so great that the actress walked off the set for a short period.

The screen treatment of this classic drama followed its stage version rather closely, deftly capturing all of Miss Hellman's bitter, tragic, and sordid undercurrents. Action was, of course, opened up somewhat from the one-set play and a new character, David Hewitt, was introduced in order to give Alexandra's departure at film's conclusion more of an uplift than had been conveyed on the stage. Gregg Toland's deep focus photography was superb.

Though the film was only moderately successful at the box office, it, Miss Davis, and Wyler received Oscar nominations, as did Teresa Wright and Patricia Collinge.

The Hubbards were too intriguing, albeit unprincipled, a family for the playwright to abandon after only one outing, so she set to work on a second

play—a prologue to *The Little Foxes* that would explore the beginnings of this clan of "spoilers." Opening in New York in 1946, *Another Part of the Forest* starred Patricia Neal, Leo Genn, Percy Waram, Mildred Dunnock, and Margaret Phillips, and was set in Alabama of 1880—two decades before the action of the earlier play.

Motion picture rights were purchased by Universal-International and assigned to produce was contractee Jerry Bresler, who recalls: "Universal flew me back to New York to see the play and, frankly, I didn't like it. The show seemed to lack clarity and didn't have a good ending. Then, when my superiors told me that Charles Coburn and Dan Duryea had been set for the two male leads, I told them I thought they were completely wrong and refused to do the project."

But the Universal brass wanted Bresler to steer this production. Thus, they agreed to let him make revisions in the script and to also recast.

"Coburn was given the lead in another Universal picture," reports Bresler, "and we replaced him with Fredric March. As for Duryea, who'd been set for

Ben, the older brother, I talked him into doing Oscar instead. That was a rather interesting piece of casting, since Duryea was now portraying the father of the character he'd played in *The Little Foxes*. Edmond O'Brien assumed the part of Ben and Ann Blyth was set for the young Regina.

"Michael Gordon directed Vladimir Pozner's screenplay, which Lillian Hellman did *not* like. In fact, I had a conversation with her prior to filming in which she stated that she would tell people she had nothing to do with the movie script. I replied that *I* would *also* let it be known that she had nothing to do with it."

Central character in this 1948 release was skinflint Marcus Hubbard (Fredric March), wealthiest and most hated man in a small Alabama community, who made his fortune as a war profiteer. His vicious family includes Regina, a shrewd little vixen, who knows how to get what she wants from the patriarch; Ben, bookkeeper in his father's store and always looking for an opportunity to steal something for himself; and Oscar, weakling youngest son, in love with a dancehall girl (Dona Drake). The sole sympathetic member of the household is Lavinia (Florence Eldridge), the mentally disturbed mother. She is the only one that knows it was her husband who, during the Civil War, turned traitor to the Confederacy, thereby causing the deaths of twenty-seven young soldiers.

When Ben learns this secret from his mother, he blackmails Marcus into turning the family treasury over to him. Both men know that, should the townsfolk learn the truth, the father would certainly be lynched for his miserable deed.

***Another Part of the Forest*. Edmond O'Brien, Fredric March, Dan Duryea, and Fritz Leiber.**

***Another Part of the Forest*. Edmond O'Brien and Fredric March.**

Ben indicates to his siblings that he intends for them to help him build a financial dynasty. Oscar will not marry his girlfriend, but, instead, will court Birdie Bagtry (Betsy Blair), whose southern aristocratic family is now land poor. Regina, spurned by Birdie's brother, military-minded John Bagtry (John Dall), now sets her sights for influential northern businessman, Horace Giddens (often discussed, but never appearing on screen).

Disgusted with her husband and the greedy opportunists she has brought into the world, Lavinia—as Alexandra would do twenty years later—walks out on her family.

One problem that Bresler realized the picture would face was the audiences' memory of the performances in *The Little Foxes*. Was it logical, for instance, that Ben, as portrayed by O'Brien, would mature into someone akin to the Charles Dingle interpretation of the same role?

***Another Part of the Forest*. Ann Blyth and Fredric March.**

On this question, the producer, wisely, followed the practical course: "I cast to the *spirit* of the original—not to the physical characteristics of the actors."

Generally speaking, the matches were good ones—O'Brien, Blyth, and Blair turning in fine performances as the young Mr. Dingle, Misses Davis and Collinge respectively. Conversely, Duryea seemed too spineless to complement Carl Benton Reid's older, more somber and calculating portrait of Oscar. Fredric March and his wife, Miss Eldridge, contributed the usual fine quality of performances which audiences had come to expect from them.

Directing Vladimir Pozner's well-fashioned screenplay, Michael Gordon seized upon every nuance of character and plot, and delivered an intense and gripping motion picture experience. The *New York Times:* "Miss Hellman has spun a fascinating drama which simmers with intrigue and conflict and explodes in a harrowing climactic burst of greed and hatreds. . . .

"While the new picture definitely doesn't have the stature of *The Little Foxes,* it is an entity in its own right and a compelling entertainment."

With the exception of time and place, Lillian Hellman's *The Little Foxes* and *Another Part of the Forest* were, in a sense, forerunners to the later works by Mario Puzo and Francis Ford Coppola—*The Godfather, Parts I and II.* Both pairs of literary endeavors dealt with evil, and how the roots of a powerful dynasty were nurtured by it. This central theme is certainly nothing new, but its presentation has seldom been as effective as when it was applied to the Hubbard and Corleone families.

## FILMOGRAPHY

1941: *Little Foxes, The* (RKO/William Wyler) Bette Davis.
1948: *Another Part of the Forest* (U/Michael Gordon) Fredric March.

# 5    *Here Comes Mr. Jordan*

When producer Everett Riskin and writer Sidney Buchman first suggested to Columbia Pictures' Harry Cohn in late 1940 that they film *Heaven Can Wait*, a play by Harry Segall, the tyrannical studio boss was a bit dubious. Traditionally, fantasy movies were bad box office, and if such presold titles like *Outward Bound* (1930) and *The Green Pastures* (1936) had failed in their screen versions, wouldn't it be rather foolish to film a story that had no reputation going for it at all?[1]

Nevertheless, Riskin and Buchman were persistent—finally getting Cohn to give the "go ahead." The men immediately began preparing their production. Seton I. Miller was set to co-author (with Buchman) the screen adaptation of the Segall play and Alexander Hall was signed to direct. To head the cast of the black-and-white production, Robert Montgomery was borrowed from Metro-Goldwyn-Mayer.

*Here Comes Mr. Jordan* (filmed under the working titles of *Heaven Can Wait* and, later, *Mr. Jordan Comes to Town*) was released during the summer of 1941. The story tells of prizefighter Joe Pendleton (Montgomery), who, prior to the crash of his light plane, is snatched from the craft by Heavenly Messenger 7013 (Edward Everett Horton) and brought before Mr. Jordan (Claude Rains) —one of God's lieutenants. Upon examination, it is discovered that Joe is not scheduled to die for another fifty years and that the overeager messenger had taken his soul prematurely. Unfortunately, Joe's body has been cremated, so it becomes Mr. Jordan's task to find the boxer another to inhabit—like a used overcoat.

Joe decides to, temporarily, assume the guise of

Bruce Farnsworth, a millionaire who has just been drowned in his bathtub by his wife, Julia (Rita Johnson), and her lover, Tony Abbott (John Emery). He does this in order to help lovely Bette Logan (Evelyn Keyes), whose father was framed by the "late" wealthy man in a stock swindle. Although, to the "living" characters in the film, Pendleton looks and sounds like Farnsworth, the audience, Jordan, and 7013 actually see him as his true self.

Having fallen in love with Bette and set Farnsworth on the road to righteousness, Joe decides to get his new body into shape in order to re-enter the fight game. He calls in Max Corkle (James Gleason), his former manager, convinces him—with some difficulty—of the truth of his unusual situation, and gets the bewildered Max to set-up a bout with K.O. Murdock, number one contender for the championship. However, later that night, he (Farnsworth) is again murdered by Julia and Tony.

Eventually, Pendleton enters Murdock's body during a championship fight, after the latter has been shot to death by gamblers wishing him to throw the contest. Joe wins the crown and Jordan, knowing that his "lost soul" is now where he belongs, erases Pendleton's memory of his former existence. All ends well when the murderers of Farnsworth are caught; Joe (as K.O.) asks Max to manage him; and Bette meets this new champion, who reminds her of someone she once knew. As Mr. Jordan had promised, Joe has gotten everything to which he was entitled.

With war clouds becoming darker every day, 1941 audiences needed a light, humorous romp like *Here Comes Mr. Jordan* to briefly take their minds off the more ominous forces surrounding them. The well-crafted piece of escapism was unanimously praised by the critics, garnered several Oscar nom-

---

1. The *Topper* series was an exception to this rule.

*Here Comes Mr. Jordan.* **Robert Montgomery and John Emery.**

*Here Comes Mr. Jordan.* **Claude Rains, Robert Montgomery, and James Gleason.**

*Here Comes Mr. Jordan.* **Robert Montgomery and Edward Everett Horton.**

inations, and became one of the big box-office grossers of the year. Perhaps the key to the film's success was best defined by the *New York Times*: "Sidney Buchman and Seton Miller, who wrote the script, and Alexander Hall, who directed it, have had the rare sense to keep the comedy where it belongs—in the characters and situations rather than in a series of double exposures and process shots of ectoplastic spooks."

It was Harry Cohn who—virtually as an afterthought—conceived the plan of having Mr. Jordan "ride again."

During the early 40s, writer Edwin Blum had set down an original story entitled "A Guy and a Goddess," which dealt with Terpsichore, the muse of song and dance, and her visit to the world of mortals. "Actually," recalls Blum, "it took me five years to develop this supernatural musical. Part of the delay came about when *One Touch of Venus* opened on Broadway. I had to rethink my story so that people wouldn't accuse me of stealing material from that show.

"Finally, after deciding that my Terpsichore would come down from the Heavens to enact herself in a play, I took the project to Harry Cohn and suggested he cast Rita Hayworth as the goddess. When I mentioned muses, Cohn lost his temper (he was always firing me) and practically threw me out of his office. 'If you think that Rita Hayworth will play a Greek,' he yelled, 'you're crazy!'

"A year or so went by. I was playing tennis with writer/producer Don Hartman and he asked me if I had a story that would be right for Rita Hayworth. I told him about 'A Guy and a Goddess.' He liked it, called Harry Cohn on the phone, and Cohn said for him to bring me right over.

"In the meantime, I'd called my agent and asked him what to do. After all, I'd already told Cohn this story and he'd refused it. But my agent said not to worry—that Cohn wouldn't remember the plot.

"Actually, I think he remembered it in his subconscious thoughts, because, as I related him the story, which I hadn't reread for some time, he would fill in small details that I'd forgotten. Yet, he didn't recall that I'd told it to him before."

Cohn liked the tale this time and made a deal for Blum to co-author the screenplay with producer Hartman. There seemed to be one major element missing from the plot: How would Terpsichore arrive on earth to become a temporary mortal?

"We'll bring back Mr. Jordan," suggested the studio chief. "He'll be the halfway point between Mt. Parnassus and Broadway."

*Down to Earth.* **Rita Hayworth and Muses.**

*Down to Earth,* as the Technicolor production was finally titled, debuted in the fall of 1947. Direction was again by Alexander Hall.

Briefly, the story tells how Terpsichore (Rita Hayworth), with the help of Mr. Jordan (played in this film by Roland Culver) and Messenger 7013 (Edward Everett Horton repeating his earlier role), journeys to Earth to portray herself in a Broadway musical about the Nine Muses of Ancient Greece. The goddess of song and dance, resentful that the production burlesques her as a modern, man-crazy hussy, has decided to show the mortals the proper way to do this play. Taking the name Kitty Pendleton, she meets Max Corkle (James Gleason again), who has left the boxing game to become a theatrical agent. He, in turn, introduces her to the producer/ star of the play, Danny Miller (Larry Parks).

When Danny's leading lady quits (with Kitty's help), the masquerading muse takes over the role and it isn't long before the guy and the goddess are in love. She later learns that Danny owes a considerable amount of money to the backer of the show, mobster Joe Mannion (George Macready). If the production flops, Danny goes for a "ride."

After Kitty's subtle attempts to give the musical more "class" nearly turns it into a disaster, she agrees to go along with Danny—back to the "jazzy" approach. The show is a hit in New York and Kitty decides she doesn't want to be a goddess. She wants to remain mortal, marry Danny, and raise a family.

Mr. Jordan appears on the scene and tells her that she must now return to Mt. Parnassus. Though she fights this inevitable fate, Jordan makes Terpsichore realize that her real purpose for being allowed to come "down to Earth"—to save Danny from Mannion's bullet—has been accomplished. The gangster has himself been murdered in a fight with his own kind.

The two supernatural beings return to Heaven and Mr. Jordan reveals to Terpsichore the future. Time is unknown in Heaven and the muse sees that it will only seem like a split-second before 1986 (the date of Danny's death) rolls around and he will join her forever.

Whereas the supernatural elements were an intregal part of *Here Comes Mr. Jordan,* they were really utilized as little more than plot devices in

43

*Down to Earth.* **Larry Parks, Rita Hayworth, and Marc Platt.**

*Down to Earth.* **Roland Culver, James Gleason, and Rita Hayworth.**

*Down to Earth.* Once Terpsichore was sent to Earth by Jordan and became "mortal," the story developed like any other musical boy-loves-girl yarn. Certainly the gangster subplot was resolved in a very orthodox manner and the occasional appearances of 7013 and

his boss did nothing but remind the audience that they were indeed watching a fantasy. Take away these scenes, make Kitty a normal, talented girl, and the basic plot structure of the film is still viable.

As he did in the earlier release, James Gleason, trying to explain to the dubious police that Mr. Jordan *does* exist, contributed the film's funniest moments

Writer Blum, however, was not too happy with some of the other casting: "I'd always wanted Rita Hayworth for the movie. In fact, the story was written with her in mind. But, I thought that Gene Kelly would have been a better choice for the male lead. Musically, he was far more talented than Parks, who, in my opinion, could only mimic Al Jolson."

*Down to Earth* was a fairly successful picture, which, for the most part, entertained its audiences. But its script was no *Here Comes Mr. Jordan,* nor did its musical sequences approach the quality of Columbia's 1946 hit, *The Jolson Story.* Said the *New York Times:* "One piece of Jordan hocus-pocus in a theatrical lifetime is nigh enough. But, at least, one more genial interference by the gentleman in *Down to Earth* . . . gets a pretty good musical underway."

Maybe if Harry Segall had been able to contribute his clever touch for comedy/fantasy to the Hayworth starrer, it might have been compared more favorably to its predecessor. On the other hand, a year earlier, this master of fantasy had authored *Angel on My Shoulder,* which had Paul Muni playing a slain gangster, brought *up* to Earth by Satan (Claude Rains as Jordan's opposite number) to do his dirty work. Though amusing, it was not a "money" film, which might indicate that fantasy movies were still, on the whole, box-office "poison."

## FILMOGRAPHY

1941: *Here Comes Mr. Jordan* (Col/Alexander Hall) Robert Montgomery.
1947: *Down to Earth* (Col/Alexander Hall) Rita Hayworth.

# 6  *Mrs. Miniver*

"Let's do something for the British. They're so badly off."

It was that thought from producer Sidney Franklin—conveyed to writer George Froeschel in mid-1941—that launched *Mrs. Miniver*, certainly one of the most popular films to emerge from Hollywood during World War II.

The extremely well-crafted screenplay by Froeschel, Arthur Wimperis, James Hilton, and Claudine West was based on a series of short narrative essays by Jan Struther, which had been published in the *London Times* and also collected into a popular book. These affectionate stories, set *prior* to the start of the world conflict, dealt with Kay and Clem Miniver—a middle-class English couple who resided with their children in a small town outside of London.

Froeschel: "Miss Struther's book was nothing more than a series of very well-written sentimental sketches that told of various incidents in the everyday life of this family. There was no continuing story line.

"It was Sidney Franklin's idea to take this typical English family that had already become known to millions of readers, and show how they and their neighbors fared in the war—particularly during the Battle of Britain."

Cast as the Minivers in the Metro-Goldwyn-Mayer production were Greer Garson and Walter Pidgeon, who'd previously co-starred together in *Blossoms in the Dust* (1941), and would go on to become one of that studio's most successful teams, appearing in such pictures as *Madame Curie* (1943), *Mrs. Parkington* (1944), and *Julia Misbehaves* (1948). Director of the project was William Wyler.

According to George Froeschel, the screenplay of *Mrs. Miniver* (1942) began in an entirely different manner than what ultimately wound-up on the screen: "We felt that audiences would need some device in order to interest them in this English-woman, so a prologue was written in which a Nazi agent, stationed in Britain, dictates a letter to his superiors in Berlin, telling them that the English will be easy to defeat because they are so superficial. He then looks out his window and sees Mrs. Miniver buying her hat.

"Wyler never shot this introduction with the spy, however, because, frankly, it wasn't needed. Instead, the first thing audiences saw was Mrs. Miniver contemplating whether she should buy the hat or not."

*Mrs. Miniver.* **Greer Garson, Christopher Seven, Walter Pidgeon, and Clare Sandars.**

Prior to the war, the Minivers are idyllically happy, residing in the country town of Belham. The family includes, besides Kay (Garson) and Clem (Pidgeon), offspring Vin (Richard Ney), an Oxford student, Judy (Clare Sandars), and Toby (Christopher Seven).

Mr. Ballard (Henry Travers), the railway station agent, is a lover of flowers and, because of his admiration for Kay, has named his new rose the "Mrs. Miniver." He causes tongues to wag by daring to enter the rose in the annual flower show given by Lady Beldon (Dame May Whitty), who's always won first prize in the contest.

When the matron's granddaughter, Carol Beldon (Teresa Wright), comes to the Miniver household to implore Kay to have Ballard's rose withdrawn, she meets Vin and they eventually fall in love.

Citizens of Belham learn by way of a church announcement from the vicar (Henry Wilcoxon), that war has been declared. Vin joins the R.A.F., then gets Carol to agree to marry him. The night of the engagement, Clem and the other men in the village collect every floatable boat to aid in rescuing

*Mrs. Miniver.* **Greer Garson and Henry Wilcoxon.**

British soldiers from the beach at Dunkirk. While he is gone, Kay encounters a wounded Nazi flier (Helmut Dantine), whom she turns over to the authorities.

Carol and Vin marry and return from their honeymoon in Scotland in time for Lady Beldon's flower show, which is won by Mr. Ballard's "Mrs. Miniver." Lady Beldon's generosity in bestowing the award on someone other than herself garners her a standing ovation from the townspeople.

*Mrs. Miniver.* **Teresa Wright and Greer Garson.**

An air raid that night claims the life of Mr. Ballard in his moment of glory. Vin returns to his base and Kay and Carol start for home. Caught in the raid, Carol dies from a stray enemy machine-gun bullet.

Next day, the village is in ruins, but in the church—with its shattered roof—the vicar gathers his congregation together to reaffirm their faith in the future.

Though definitely war propaganda, *Mrs. Miniver* was a fine motion picture, an admirable blend of light and humor, pathos and tragedy. Performances were faultless, with all actors realizing the full potential of their particular roles.

*Variety:* "In the production by Sidney Franklin, the direction by William Wyler, the unaffected performances by Greer Garson and Walter Pidgeon and their scarcely subordinate peers, an extraordinary amount of taste, discretion, and artistry has been displayed to make this one of the most important and beautiful film dramas of the season."

Franklin's production realized a gross domestic film rental of $5.5 million, and won Oscars for Best Picture, Director, Actress (Garson), Supporting Actress (Wright), Screenplay, and Cinematography.

**The Miniver Story. Richard Gale, Greer Garson, and Walter Pidgeon.**

George Froeschel: "*Mrs. Miniver* was such a success that, for years, Sidney Franklin pursued me to write a sequel, but I avoided it. Finally, the studio set Ronald Millar to do this follow-up story, however, after three months, he announced that a sequel was impossible. At that point, Franklin asked me to take over the script as a favor to him, so I did."

Whereas the original picture had been shot at MGM in Hollywood, *The Miniver Story* (1950) was filmed on location in England, under the direction of H. C. Potter. Reprising their original roles were Miss Garson, Pidgeon, Wilcoxon, and Reginald Owen, who'd played "Foley," the village grocer. Noticeably absent was Richard Ney as Vin.

Following the completion of *Mrs. Miniver*, Ney and Greer Garson were married, but had since divorced. To avoid what might become a difficult situation between those players during filming, the studio decided it would be better if the eldest son were written out of the story and, therefore, the script had him "killed in action."

The Millar/Froeschel screenplay is set after the war, when we learn, via a doctor, that Mrs. Miniver has only a short time to live. Thereafter, the saga chiefly concerns itself with her efforts to straighten out certain family problems in the brief period allotted to her.

The Miniver Story. Greer Garson and John Hodiak.

She breaks up a romance between now-grown daughter Judy (Cathy O'Donnell) and a married man (Leo Genn), then gives her approval when Tom Foley (Richard Gale), the grocer's son, proposes to the young girl; deals with the unexpected declaration of love for her by an American Air Force colonel (John Hodiak); and helps husband Clem overcome his postwar restlessness that takes the form of his wanting to move to Brazil. At the picture's conclusion, Kay Miniver can expire in peace, knowing full well that, through her manipulations, her loved ones will be able to carry on without her.

Froeschel: "The basic idea for the movie—that of Mrs. Miniver being terminally ill and keeping it to herself—was lousy, and the production it received didn't help matters. The family seemed completely different from the original movie. It was a very slow and dull film."

Indeed, The Miniver Story was both a critical and box-office disaster. Variety commented: "Story is patently a contrived effort to cash in on the great

The Miniver Story. Greer Garson and Walter Pidgeon.

48

humanness of the foregoing picture. Instead of projecting former film's warmness and fine feeling again, however, *Story* is a maudlin pitch at audience's emotional sensitivities and misses honest drama."

The talented cast tried their best to bring some life to the soggy script, but, as the *New York Times* observed: "The only poignant thing about this picture is the reduction to such a sorry state of a character whom we hold in special memory. It is just as well that she has died."

Mr. Froeschel, a fugitive from Hitler's Germany, is amused by the fact that, during the war, Nazi propagandist Joseph Goebbels screened *Mrs. Miniver* for his staff on numerous occasions, informing them: "This is how a propaganda picture *should* look!"

## FILMOGRAPHY

1942: *Mrs. Miniver* (MGM/William Wyler) Greer Garson.

1950: *Miniver Story, The* (MGM/H. C. Potter) Greer Garson.

# 7    *The Jolson Story*

***The Jolson Story*. Larry Parks.**

He was a titan . . . the "world's greatest entertainer" . . . a legend in his own time. A man who could make the lyrics of any song into his own personal property, he had captured and held Broadway for years, then starred in the screen's first talking picture. And yet, as far as the show business community was concerned, by the mid-1940s, Al Jolson was an anachronism. His style, compared to then-modern idols like Sinatra, had dated. As they say in the trade, "he couldn't get himself arrested."

Two men—columnist Sidney Skolsky and Columbia Pictures head Harry Cohn—came to Jolie's rescue.

The chronicler of Hollywood happenings had been trying to peddle a film biography of the mammy-singer—without his subject's knowledge—for some time, but had received negative responses from every studio. When Cohn, an avid fan of Jolson's, learned of the idea, he immediately sent for Skolsky and, after hearing his plan to have another actor "mouth" Al's singing voice, agreed to finance the project. Jolson, whose ego equaled his talent, was, of course, not hard to sell (his radio series had recently been cancelled), agreeing to accept fifty percent of the movie's profits (in lieu of an advance), plus twenty-five thousand dollars for recording the songs. Although his superiors in New York were against this film—feeling that Jolson was a "has-been"—Cohn was determined the near three million dollar-budgeted picture would be a success.

Speculation in "tinsel-town" mounted as to who would play the ex-blackfaced minstrel, who was too old to portray himself. First choice James Cagney refused the bid because, after *Yankee Doodle Dandy* (1942), in which he'd essayed George M. Cohan, he was not interested in doing the role of another show business immortal. Newcomer Danny Thomas also

nixed the assignment when he learned that Cohn was insisting that he submit to a "nose-job." Richard Conte and Jose Ferrer were others considered.

The only actor to be tested for the part was Larry Parks, whose previous work had consisted, primarily, of secondary roles in B pictures. Although he, physically, looked nothing like the singer, Cohn, Skolsky, and, ultimately, Jolson agreed that Parks had captured Al's performing style to the point where the resemblance was uncanny. The assignment was his.

From the outset, it had been agreed that *The Jolson Story* (1946) would *not* be a *definitive* biography. Actually, with the exception of touching upon some of the highlights of the entertainer's life, the bulk of Stephen Longstreet's screenplay, from an adaptation by Harry Chandlee and Andrew Solt,

**The Jolson Story. Larry Parks, William Demarest, Bill Goodwin, Evelyn Keyes.**

was fiction. Ignored was Jolson's stormy relationship with his rabbi father; the existence of his brother, Harry (with whom he was feuding); and his first two marriages. Since ex-wife Ruby Keeler refused to allow the use of her name in the production, this character, played by Evelyn Keyes, had her moniker changed to "Julie Benson."

However, the most important modification of reality was in the interpretation of Jolson himself. Possessing a personality that left much to be desired (many of his contemporaries considered him to be an "abusive son-of-a-bitch"), the singer was, nevertheless, portrayed by Parks as a rather likable, if bland, sort, whose first and only true love was show business.

Producer Skolsky and Cohn felt the public didn't

care that much about Jolson's less than virtuous life, but would, instead, pay the price of admission just to hear him sing the wonderful songs he had immortalized. As it turned out, they were right.

Directed by Alfred E. Green, the Technicolor film begins in Washington, D.C. at the turn of the century. Twelve-year-old Asa Yoelson (Scotty Beckett), son of a cantor (Ludwig Donath), skips services to sing in a burlesque house. He is seen by comedian Steve Martin (William Demarest), who goes to his father and mother (Tamara Shayne) to request that the lad be allowed to join his act. Cantor Yoelson is horrified at the thought of his son going with a theatrical troupe and refuses, but the boy runs away from home and, after he is picked up by the police, father agrees to entrust his child to the vaudevillian.[1]

1. In reality, Jolson had begun his show business career in a vaudeville act with his brother, Harry.

*The Jolson Story.* **Larry Parks, Bill Goodwin, and William Demarest.**

*The Jolson Story.* **Larry Parks and Evelyn Keyes.**

Over the next few years, Asa, who eventually changes his name to Al Jolson (Parks), travels with Martin and perfects his talent. Lew Dockstader (John Alexander), the famous minstrel man, spots the artist in a performance and, with Steve's help, lures him into joining his show. When he outgrows Dockstader, Jolson is called upon by producer/friend Tom Baron (Bill Goodwin) to appear in a New York show for the Shuberts. In blackface, singing "Mammy," Al is a sensation, and quickly rises to stardom on Broadway. He does one successful production after another at the Winter Garden Theater, feeding on the thunderous applause of his audiences.

After he hires an "at liberty" Steve Martin as his manager, Jolson signs to star in the first talking picture, *The Jazz Singer*. However, before leaving for the West Coast, he meets Flo Ziegfeld's new musical comedy star, Julie Benson. It is love at first sight. A few months later, the couple marry and move to Los Angeles.

Julie longs for a life away from the hustle and bustle of the entertainment world, but realizes that

Al thrives on this kind of activity. Jolson tries to quit, yet is miserable in his retirement. When an offer arrives for him to star in a new Broadway show, Julie walks out on her husband—as he sings impromptu in a nightclub—because she knows that maintaining the marriage will only destroy them both.

Henry Levin, who directed the sequel to *The Jolson Story, Jolson Sings Again,* recalls a visit he paid to the set of the original picture: "Larry Parks was excellent in mimicking Jolson's singing style. He accomplished this with a lot of practice, and by having the sound man turn the music up to the point where he couldn't hear *himself* singing.

"I think that Jolson was actually jealous, because Parks was in front of the camera and he wasn't. He was such an egotist that he wanted to be on all the time. In fact, while the crew was lighting the Winter Garden set, Al got up on stage and entertained the extras for the better part of an hour."

Even Harry Cohn was surprised when *The Jolson Story* garnered a domestic gross of eight million dollars. The picture made a star of Larry Parks and catapulted Jolson back to the show business heights he'd enjoyed in the twenties. After the release of this flawed, but pleasing—primarily because of its musical sequences—production, Al truly became the "hottest" property in the industry.

*Variety* called it "one of the top musicals of the screen. Film catches the spirit of the man Jolson and what he stands for in world of entertainment. . . ."

The *New York Times,* though disappointed with the movie's syrupy treatment of Jolson's life, did find the production to be an audibly enjoyable experience, commenting: ". . . *The Jolson Story* is more a phonographic than photographic job."

One of the film's major disappointments was the omission of a Jolson classic, "Sonny Boy." That number had originally been included in the production, but Cohn had it removed after he decided it slowed the pace of the 126-minute musical.

Sidney Buchman both wrote and produced the 1949 sequel, *Jolson Sings Again,* a project that, though conceived shortly after the success of the parent picture was assured, was not easy to launch.

For well over a year, a number of rumors and half-truths made the rounds in Hollywood: Jolson wanted to make the picture at MGM with Gene Kelly in the lead; the entertainer wanted to play himself this time out; or Larry Parks was refusing to do the sequel.

Eventually, all matters were settled amicably.

Jolson decided that it was not wise to fool around with a successful formula and agreed to let Columbia do the picture with Parks, who'd garnered an Oscar nomination for the 1946 effort. The young actor, on the other hand, was given a new, more advantageous, contract by the studio, which allowed him to do outside pictures.[2] William Demarest, Ludwig Donath, Bill Goodwin, and Tamara Shayne were also signed to reprise their respective roles.

Again filmed in Technicolor, this Henry Levin-directed movie picked up the Jolson saga immediately following the conclusion of its predecessor—with Al learning that Julie has left him. Steve Martin urges his friend to accept Tom Baron's offer to star once more on Broadway, which Jolson does and is a smash hit. But, when Julie files for divorce, Al decides to quit show business, because the "kick" is gone.

Following the death of his mother and the outbreak of the Second World War, Jolson is the first entertainer to offer his services to the USO. He tirelessly performs for troops all over the world—in the Pacific, Africa, Italy—until he collapses from the strain. Ultimately, his ceaseless efforts to do something for the serviceman results in the removal of a lung.

Jolson's hospital stays have resulted in his meeting nurse Ellen Clark[3] (Barbara Hale), whom he eventually marries. Unlike Julie, Ellen urges Al to re-enter show business, because she knows it is the only thing that will make him truly happy. Producers, regrettably, consider the performer washed up and getting him work is not easy—until he appears at the bottom of the bill at a Hollywood Community Chest benefit.

Seated in the audience is a movie producer (Myron McCormick), who approaches Al with the idea of filming *The Jolson Story.* The remainder of the picture deals with the production of this phenomenal hit, which, again, makes Jolie the "king of show business."

In certain respects, *Jolson Sings Again* was a superior production to the 1946 musical. Its screenplay was tighter, less episodic, and, though still coming off as "Mr. Nice-Guy," the Jolson characterization—as essayed by Parks—seemed much more human this time. Certainly the dramatic story of a once-successful entertainer trying to regain his former glory gave the actor more viable material to

2. Parks's promising career would be destroyed in the early fifties, after he appeared before the Un-American Activities Committee.
3. Her real name was Erle Galbraith.

53

*Jolson Sings Again.* Larry Parks, Ludwig Donath, Barbara Hale, and William Demarest.

*Jolson Sings Again.* Larry Parks, William Demarest, Myron McCormick, and players.

work with than he'd had in the earlier film, which was really quite superficial in its plot development. Veritably, Buchman's combining a little vinegar with the sugar resulted in a much stronger biography.

An amusing feature in the movie was a double-exposed scene in which Parks, as Jolson, meets Parks, as Parks, the actor who would impersonate him in the vehicle that would revive his career.

*Variety* said: "The Sidney Buchman production is a rare thing in motion picture annals. A follow-up that matches, maybe even surpasses the first. What *The Jolson Story* had in abundance, *Jolson Sings Again* doubles in spades."

Though the 1949 release grossed only five million dollars in domestic rentals, it was still a major success, since its cost was less than two million.

Undeniably, the Jolson pictures and *Yankee Doodle Dandy* are among the most popular film biographies in history. Each is a romanticized version of the life of a show business giant, who, in reality, was *not* a "very nice person." Considering George C. Scott's brutally frank portrayal of Patton in 1970, it might be rather interesting from a dramatic, if not nostalgic, standpoint to redo these two earlier movie biographies, utilizing a more honest approach. If nothing else, such projects would certainly give a couple of actors some rather meaty material to work with.[4]

## FILMOGRAPHY

1946: *Jolson Story, The* (Col/Alfred E. Green) Larry Parks.

1949: *Jolson Sings Again* (Col/Henry Levin) Larry Parks.

4. In 1968, Joel Grey starred in *George M*, a relatively factual Broadway musical based on the life of George M. Cohan. Whereas the play was later done as a television special, it has never been filmed for cinema audiences.

# 8 The Paleface

As a stand-up comedian, Bob Hope has no equal. Old "ski-nose" is readily acknowledged by his peers —indeed, the English-speaking world—as the ranking court jester for any number of statesmen, presidents, and royalty, not to mention thousands of American servicemen in foreign lands. His television specials consistently garner high ratings . . . and he makes movies.

It is within this last field of endeavor that the beloved-by-millions entertainer has sometimes floundered. Whereas many of his film vehicles have reaped respectable financial rewards at the box office (none were blockbusters, however), few of these productions have been able to retain their humor over the years. Saddled with weak story lines, the comedies relied heavily on inferior slapstick material and, more importantly, a string of rapid, contemporary visual and verbal gags from the star, which tended to date the pictures rather quickly. Today, even the low-brow routines ("Who's on First") from early Abbott and Costello films seem more timeless in their entertainment value than Hope's product of a decade later.[1]

Nevertheless, he *has* provided some amusing moments of screen hilarity. The *Road* pictures, for example, with Bing Crosby and Dorothy Lamour, though somewhat antiquated like Hope's other efforts, are still considered classics—primarily because of the relaxed rivalry between the comic and the crooner.

From the standpoint of box office, Hope's most successful non-*Road* picture was the 1948 Technicolor comedy, *The Paleface*, a Paramount release,

co-starring Jane Russell. Repeating his usual screen characterization—the likable coward who comes out on top either through luck or by using his wits, the comedian played "Painless" Peter Potter, a bumbling Eastern dentist, earning his living by treating frontiersmen. Lovely outlaw Calamity Jane (Russell), working for the government in order to gain a pardon, marries the naive Potter as part of her plan to capture a gang of smugglers who are selling arms to rampaging Indians. In an attack by the red men, Jane makes it appear that the dentist is a hero (*she* shoots the Indians, while he hides in a barrel—firing at the ground) and this ruse aids considerably in finally bringing the heavies to justice. At the film's conclusion, the pistol-packing lady realizes that she actually loves the klutz she's married.

Directed by Norman Z. McLeod, from a script by Edmund Hartmann and Frank Tashlin (additional dialogue was credited to Jack Rose), *The Paleface* delighted audiences through Hope's unending barrage of topical one-liners and sexual innuendos aimed at Miss Russell. In one running gag, she would strike her husband (in name only) on the head with a gun-butt every time they kissed, so that she could attend to her undercover work alone.

Highlight of the picture was the Jay Livingston and Ray Evans tune (sung by Hope) "Buttons and Bows," which went on to win the Academy Award.

The *New York Times*: ". . . a second string *Road* show, at best, conspicuously lacking the presence of Bing Crosby and Dorothy Lamour. . . .

"*The Paleface* deserves primarily a marker as the birthplace of 'Buttons and Bows.'"

As is often the case, the public paid scant attention to reviews like the above. Domestic box-office gross for the picture totaled $4.5 million.

---

1. Most durable are Hope's *Sorrowful Jones* (1949), *The Seven Little Foys* (1955), *Beau James* (1957), and *The Facts of Life* (1960), all of which sacrificed the one-liners in favor of a stronger screenplay.

*The Paleface.* Bob Hope and Jane Russell.

*The Paleface.* Jane Russell and Bob Hope.

*The Paleface.* Bob Hope and Iron Eyes Cody.

1952 found Hope and the powers at Paramount capitalizing on their 1948 hit by producing *Son of Paleface*.[2] The Technicolor film was helmed by Frank Tashlin (his directing debut), who also co-authored the script with producer Robert L. Welch and Joseph Quillan. Again, Jane Russell co-starred and, this time, Roy Rogers, "King of the Cowboys," and his horse, Trigger, were along for the ride.

The plot had Junior Potter (Hope), a Harvard graduate, leaving school to travel West to reclaim his late father's fortune. A coward like his old man, he meets up with Rogers (playing himself) who, assuming the guise of a medicine showman, is out to catch "The Torch" (Russell), and her gang of gold shipment bandits. The femme outlaw's alternate identity is that of Mike, a saloon entertainer/owner.

Junior learns that his father had hidden his treasure, a situation which creates problems for him, since Daddy owed much money to the townspeople of Sawbuck Pass, who now want to lynch the younger Potter. With the aid of Rogers, he is able to find the gold—in a neighboring ghost town. Then, the pair—helped by Mike, who has decided to "go straight"—capture the gang of criminals. Marrying Junior, the shapely outlaw troops off to prison—only to be released some time later with a band of little Potters tagging along. As Junior comments, "Let's see television top this!"

*Son of Paleface* had some great gags[3]—many of which were directed at Rogers and his screen image of the clean-living cowboy. In one scene, Hope asks the westerner, who had been oblivious to the attention Russell had showered upon him, if he liked girls. Replies Roy: "I prefer horses, Mister."

Another sequence involved Hope driving his automobile through the desert and being visited by a pair of buzzards, whom he refers to as "Martin and Lewis."

The *New York Times* liked this effort better than the first: ". . . what is delivered in this colored package is a wild farce that comes so close to the style of those old *Road to ———* pictures of Mr. Hope, Bing Crosby and Dorothy Lamour that you might almost shut your eyes (if you can manage) and think you are enjoying one of the same."

In February of 1955, the California State District Court of Appeals upheld a Superior Court verdict in favor of Paramount Pictures, in a six hundred

2. Plotwise, there was little to connect the two pictures beyond the fact that the characters Hope played in both movies shared a blood relationship. Sans the presold title, one would never have known he was watching a sequel.
3. Cecil B. DeMille appeared as photographer Matthew Brady.

thousand dollar suit brought by Freddie Rich involving the song, "Buttons and Bows." Rich had alleged plagiarism, stating that a passage from the tune was copied from a song he'd written as music for another Paramount release. Paramount had, successfully, claimed the controversial music phrase was used in traditional folk music.

Although both *The Paleface* and *Son of Paleface* can still evoke an occasional smile from modern audiences, these reactions are nothing like the tremendous belly-laughs that were brought forth when they were originally released well over two decades ago. Because of their now outdated gags, the previously successful pictures are, today, best regarded academically—as prime examples of Bob Hope's choice humor (*circa* 1948–52).

## FILMOGRAPHY

1948: *Paleface, The* (Par/Norman Z. McLeod) Bob Hope.
1952: *Son of Paleface* (Par/Frank Tashlin) Bob Hope.

*Son of Paleface.* **Jane Russell, Roy Rogers, and Bob Hope.**

*Son of Paleface.* **Douglass Dumbrille, Bob Hope, and Roy Rogers.**

# 9  *Broken Arrow*

"The only *good* Indian is a *dead* Indian" is the familiar slogan that most aptly describes the movies' attitude toward the red man during the 1930s and 40s. Filmgoers of that era, whose knowledge of history was limited to what they saw on the theater screen, came to believe that the American Indian was a blood-thirsty savage, who spent all his time chasing stagecoaches, burning farmhouses, and torturing innocent women and children. John Wayne and Errol Flynn, both of whom could slay a half-dozen of these beasts with one bullet, became the nation's heroes. After all, the West could never have been settled safely without them.

*Broken Arrow*, released in 1950 by Twentieth Century-Fox, was the first major picture to discard the stereotype and present its Indian characters as human beings—members of an ancient and honorable race whose primitive intellect was equal to any civilized culture, not merely in matters of conflict, but in social structure, community service, and morality.

For producer Julian Blaustein, formerly an editorial supervisor with David O. Selznick, the film was the realization of a two-year dream. He'd long been intrigued by *Blood Brother*, a novel by Elliott Arnold, but was aware that every major studio had turned it down—probably because of its anticipated high budget. Nevertheless, Blaustein studied the work, which dealt with Cochise, the Chief of the Chiricahua Apaches who led his people in war against the United States for nearly eleven years, and, after developing a screen treatment, took an option on it. He hired Michael Blankfort to write a script, then, when that was ready, presented it to actor James Stewart—his first choice for the leading role of Tom Jeffords, the frontiersman who is tired of the senseless killings. In the novel, this character didn't appear until the halfway point, but Blankfort's version had him in from the start as narrator.

Blaustein discussed his picture in a 1950 interview with the *Los Angeles Times:* "My chief objective was to get the story made honestly and, colloquially speaking, properly. I could have done it independently at any of three studios, but decided in favor of coming to Fox where, happily, Darryl Zanuck liked the script and the idea of having Stewart in the lead.

"What we hoped to do was to bring a documentary approach to a historical subject. By using unfamiliar faces in all except the Jeffords part, we might make them acceptable as human beings.

"When I say 'them,' I mean the Apache Indians

***Broken Arrow*. Jeff Chandler as Cochise.**

59

*Broken Arrow.* Jeff Chandler, Basil Ruysdael, and James Stewart.

*Broken Arrow.* James Stewart and Jeff Chandler.

who were in conflict with the white men in the 1870s. We wanted to deal with Indians who would not look like cardboard cutouts of red men, and particularly with Cochise, the chief, who, besides being a fearless warrior, was also a man of vision and feeling. Jeffords, the white man, was lifted by his association with him.

"We have treated them [the Indians] as people, not savages; have tried to show that the only real 'heavies' are ignorance, misunderstanding, and intolerance.

"In short, none of our Indians say 'Ugh!' "

The Technicolor production, filmed in Arizona where the story actually took place during the 1860s and 70s, tells of how ex-Army scout Jeffords took the first step to end the ongoing war between the Apaches and whites. He'd had an enlightening confrontation with the red men at the start of the movie in which the braves, after brutally killing a band of prospectors, spared his life because he'd nursed an injured Indian youth back to health. This taught him that Apaches had a sense of fair play.

Jeffords learns the Chiricahua language, then journeys alone to Cochise's mountain stronghold for a parley with the chief (Jeff Chandler). As a peace gesture, the Indian leader, who has been taught through experience that whites never keep their treaties, agrees to allow Pony Express riders from Tucson to pass safely through Apache country. This, eventually, leads to a meeting with General O. O. Howard (Basil Ruysdael), a representative of President Grant. The one-armed military man has been authorized to negotiate an armistice with Cochise, which, after days of conferences with other Apache chiefs, is signed. Only the renegade Geronimo (Jay Silverheels) and his small band of followers dissent and walk away. Later, the now-peaceful Chiricahuas—guaranteed their exclusive territory—fight Geronimo when he attacks a stagecoach.

Jeffords and Cochise have become close friends and, when the white man asks permission to marry Sonseeahray (Debra Paget), an Indian maiden, the chief gives his blessing. The couple's happiness is short-lived, however. White bigots, led by Ben Slade (Will Geer), kill Jeffords's wife during an unsuccessful attempt to assassinate Cochise. These killers are either shot down or captured and the peace treaty remains in force.

Though the basic facts in *Broken Arrow* are essentially correct, Blaustein did take some dramatic license. The real Jeffords, for example, met and befriended Cochise in 1862, but the meeting with General Howard did not take place until 1871. The film telescopes these, as well as other events, so that they all seemingly occur within a matter of months. Also, whereas there is evidence that Jeffords did have a woman in the Indian camp, his romance with Sonseeahray was fiction.

Reviews for this Delmer Daves-directed picture were on two levels. Most critics praised the offbeat western. *Variety:* "Picture, excellently mounted, displays top-rank efforts of producer Julian Blaustein, director Delmer Daves, and scripter Michael Blankfort. Latter has provided a suspenseful and action-crammed layout, accentuated by skillful piloting by Daves, and crisp editing. . . .

"Stewart is outstanding, but must share top honors with Chandler and Miss Paget. Chandler, with a strong physique dominating personality, is a candidate for fast buildup to stellar ranking."

Beautifully photographed against the Arizona landscape by Ernest Palmer, the Fox production was a rare and exciting motion picture, which gave audiences a sympathetic look at a people who had previously been the screen's most dastardly villains. No boring message film was this, but one that made its point while still providing viewers with real, compelling, and vigorous entertainment.

Conversely, while giving the movie a strong nod for its noble intent, some chroniclers commented that the depiction of Indians in *Broken Arrow* was too unrealistic and that the death of Jeffords's wife was an unnecessary gesture to satisfy the bigots in the audience who could not accept the miscegenation element. The *New York Times:* "But apparently in his enthusiasm to treat the Indian with politeness and respect, Delmer Daves, the director, brought forth red men who act like denizens of the musical comedy stage. Jeff Chandler, who plays Cochise, is twice as clean and stalwart-looking as James Stewart, who plays the drawling prospector by whom the peaceful mission is embarked. Mr. Chandler carries himself with the magnificence of a decathalon champion at the Olympic Games and speaks with the round and studied phrasing of the salutatorian of a graduating class. . . .

"No, we cannot accept this picture as either an exciting or reasonable account of the attitudes and ways of American Indians. They merit justice, but not such patronage."

As a result of his powerful portrayal of Cochise, Jeff Chandler received an Oscar nomination in the supporting actor category and, of more importance, was elevated to stardom. Unfortunately, being under contract to Universal-International, who'd loaned him to Fox for the James Stewart topliner, he now found himself cast by his home studio in a series of low-grade program efforts, which did nothing but diminish the box-office appeal he'd achieved.

*Broken Arrow.* James Stewart and Debra Paget.

*The Battle at Apache Pass.* Jeff Chandler, Regis Toomey, and John Lund.

Director George Sherman reflects: "I'd really 'discovered' Jeff when I cast him in *Sword in the Desert*, the movie that got him considered for *Broken Arrow*. Shortly after the Fox picture was released and garnered a sensational reaction from the public, I had the opportunity to leave Universal (where I was under contract) and go over to Metro to direct Gable in *Lone Star*. But, instead, I chose to stay where I was and direct Jeff again, who I thought was on the verge of becoming a *major* star."

Always ready to sieze a golden opportunity, the Universal brass had decided that Chandler should released and garnered a sensational reaction from the Cavalry officer; the hanging of his brother under the banner. The actor was, after all, their property and, perhaps, a repeat performance of his best-known role would cause box-office lightning to strike again —this time for Universal. Set to develop the project with Sherman were producers Leonard Goldstein and Ross Hunter. Gerald Drayson Adams scripted.

Chandler initially balked at the idea of repeating Cochise, but when Sherman explained that he'd turned down a Gable film in order to work with him, he acquiesced.

Historically, the *true* events depicted in *The Battle at Apache Pass* (1952) took place at the time of the Civil War, *prior* to the action in *Broken Arrow*. At the start of the picture, Cochise (Chandler played the part much younger this time out) and his people are friendly to the whites and the Apache chief enjoys a close relationship with Major Colton (John Lund), commandant of a New Mexico outpost. The renegade Geronimo (Jay Silverheels, again) causes some trouble, but the settlers in the area realize that most of the Indians wish to live in peace.

Serious problems erupt when Neil Baylor (Bruce Cowling), a crooked Government Indian Adviser who plots to take over the lush Apache lands, makes a secret pact with Geronimo to supply the banished chief with guns if he will execute a massacre and make it appear that Cochise was responsible. Baylor then takes advantage of Colton's absence by duping the eager, but inexperienced, Lt. Bascom (John Hudson) into attacking Cochise. Ignoring a flag of peace, Bascom hangs Cochise's brother and two of his cousins, enraging the chief to lead all the Apache tribes in a campaign to annihilate the whites.

The climax of the film comes when Colton, in evacuating his fort, leads his party through Apache Pass and is attacked by the now-allied Cochise and Geronimo. The Cavalry turns the tide in their favor when they invoke the use of artillery—the first time Apaches have seen such weapons.

Nona (Susan Cabot), Cochise's wife, goes into labor during the battle and, under a white flag, the chief brings the woman to an Army doctor. Geronimo violates the temporary truce, but Cochise rides out to meet him in hand-to-hand combat. Defeating the rebel, he refuses to slay him, sending him away in disgrace. At picture's end, Cochise, his family, and braves withdraw, promising to consider the possibilities of peace.

George Sherman: "Much of what we portrayed in the picture was true—Cochise's friendship with the Cavalry officer; the hanging of his brother under the white flag; and, of course, the battle of Apache Pass itself. However, to make the story work dramatically, we did bring in some fiction: Cochise's wife did not give birth on the battlefield (in truth, the Apaches, not knowing how to cope with artillery, simply withdrew), nor was the Indian adviser a real character. On the other hand, there's plenty of evidence to prove that many of these government officials were, indeed, corrupt."

Shot at Moab, Utah, in Technicolor, *The Battle*

*Taza, Son of Cochise.* **Rock Hudson and Jeff Chandler.**

*Taza, Son of Cochise.* **Rock Hudson and Ian MacDonald.**

*at Apache Pass* made an honest attempt to show the basic events that ignited the bloody Apache War. Again, the Indians were presented sympathetically, but, in this instance, some two-dimensional characterizations and the introduction of melodramatic elements—such as the government adviser's treachery—helped to reduce the final result to what might best be called a very good *program* western—definitely not in the same league with its predecessor, *Broken Arrow.*

The *Hollywood Reporter:* "Sherman is particularly successful in establishing an over-all mood so that while the film is a lively one, underneath all the excitement there is always subtly registered the tragedy of the Indians doomed by the inexorable progress of the white man and forced to yield to his encroachments. . . .

"Chandler does a splendid job as Cochise, playing him with sensitivity and dignity."

More demanding papers like the *New York Times* judged the production with greater severity: "Some of the terrible irony of this ancient conflict does

63

manage to filter through all the dust and commotion, but principally when the magnificent Technicolored scenery reduces the participants to mere specks on the horizon."

Inspired by the financial success of their film, Universal decided that a sequel was in order and, early in 1954, released the 3-D/Technicolor epic, *Taza, Son of Cochise*, which had contract player Rock Hudson playing the offspring of the great chief, who was, once more, portrayed (unbilled) by Chandler—in a single scene.

At his father's deathbed, Taza promises he will try to keep the peace that Cochise had painstakingly made with the whites. The villain is, again, Geronimo (Ian MacDonald), who comes to the San Carlos reservation, where Taza captains an Apache police force, to seek temporary haven. The youngest son of Cochise (Bart Roberts) joins the renegade chief and, together with their braves, nearly wipe out a U.S. Cavalry column. Happily, Taza comes to the rescue and changes the tide of battle, thereby restoring peace to the territory.

Ross Hunter produced this western, which had Douglas Sirk directing an uninspired screenplay by George Zuckerman, based on a story-adaptation by Gerald Drayson Adams. Though enhanced by striking Moab, Utah, scenery and acceptable production values, the picture was hampered with the familiar Indians vs. U.S. Cavalry plot and, after a quick playoff in general runs, disappeared from theater screens.

Regarding the film's star, *Variety* said: "Rock Hudson suffices in action demands of his role of Taza, but character is never too believable."

More true to the concept originally expressed in Julien Blaustein's memorable 1950 western was the successful "Broken Arrow" television series, debuting in 1956, which Twentieth Century-Fox produced for ABC. John Lupton and Michael Ansara starred in that above-average show, deftly essaying the roles created by Stewart and Chandler respectively and, because of the magic of that electronic medium, are, today, better identified with those characterizations than their motion picture counterparts.

The argument presented for the American Indian in *Broken Arrow* and its sequels may have been overstated, but, at least, it was a step in a positive direction—leading, ultimately, to such thoughtful productions as *Run of the Arrow* (1957), *Cheyenne Autumn* (1964), *Soldier Blue* (1970), *A Man Called Horse* (1970), and *Little Big Man* (1970).

## FILMOGRAPHY

1950: *Broken Arrow* (Fox/Delmer Daves) James Stewart.
1952: *Battle at Apache Pass, The* (U/George Sherman) Jeff Chandler.
1954: *Taza, Son of Cochise* (U/Douglas Sirk) Rock Hudson.

# 10 *Cheaper by the Dozen*

Whereas the Hubbards of *The Little Foxes* may have been one of the most merciless households to ever adorn the motion picture screen, the Gilbreth clan from *Cheaper by the Dozen* was certainly the most endearing. Based on the 1949 best-selling book of the same name by Frank B. Gilbreth, Jr., and Ernestine Gilbreth Carey (two of the narrative's grown children), this delightful, sentimental comedy starred Clifton Webb as the eccentric industrial engineer patriarch of twelve offspring.

During the early 1920s, Frank Bunker Gilbreth, Sr., was, in fact, a top man in his field—famous for his innovative motion studies—while his wife, Dr. Lillian M. Gilbreth, made her place as an eminent psychologist and lecturer. When they were married, the couple decided at the outset they would have twelve babies—because they "come cheaper by the dozen." The family resided in Montclair, New Jersey, spending their blissful summers at The Shoe on Nantucket Island, Massachusetts.

Twentieth Century-Fox snapped up the movie rights (for one hundred thousand dollars) to this humorous chronicle of American family life, then set Lamar Trotti to both script and produce, and Walter Lang to direct the Technicolor adaptation, released in 1950.

The episodic screenplay begins with Gilbreth (Webb) informing his wife, Lillian (Myrna Loy) and children, including eldest daughters Anne (Jeanne Crain) and Ernestine (Barbara Bates), that the household is moving their residence from Providence, Rhode Island, to Montclair—via a 1917 Pierce Arrow touring car, dubbed "Foolish Carriage."[1]

1. The studio had considerable trouble locating an automobile of this make and vintage. According to director Lang: "The more we hunted, the more desperate we became. The catch was that we had to have one in excellent condition—at least, good enough so that we could make it look new. We found quite a few old wrecks, but none in top running order until we located a Model 48 in Berkeley, California. Actually, we had more trouble casting the car—one of the star characters in the book—than we did any of the roles."

Settled in their new home, we see that Dad insists on applying scientific reasoning to everyday situations—discussing educational subjects at dinner because "there is no reason we shouldn't take advantage of the delay to learn something of value." He refuses son William's (Jimmy Hunt) request for a dog "because any pet which doesn't lay eggs is an extravagance," and, later, demonstrates the efficient way of devouring an apple, "beginning at the North Pole and eating straight down to the South Pole."

From time-to-time, family councils are called in order to organize the work around the house. It is at one of these meetings that the clever William incites a "mutiny" and gets his fellow siblings and Mother to vote against Gilbreth on the matter of a dog. Once in the house, the pooch, naturally, adopts Father as his favorite human.

A physician insists on removing everyone's tonsils —including Dad's, who takes advantage of the mass extractions by having a motion picture cameraman film them "so we can show these doctors how they can speed things up by eliminating a lot of wasted motions." Groggily emerging from his own operation, Gilbreth learns that his efforts have been

*Cheaper By the Dozen.* **Myrna Loy, Barbara Bates, Clifton Webb, and Jeanne Crain.**

*Cheaper By the Dozen.* Mary Field, Jeanne Crain, Jimmy Hunt, and players.

*Cheaper By the Dozen.* Clifton Webb, Myrna Loy, Jimmy Hunt, Barbara Bates, and players.

wasted, since he'd forgotten to load film into the camera.

Anne rebels against her father's strict, if loving, ways by bobbing her hair. Invited to a dance, Gilbreth allows her to go—only with himself along as chaperone—and, once there, *he* becomes the lion of the evening. Anne sees her father in a new perspective when her football hero boyfriend (Craig Hill) says: "I think your father's swell coming here like this just to look after you."

Summoned to Europe in 1924 to deliver two very important lectures on his motion studies, Gilbreth dies of a heart attack at the Montclair railroad station.

Mother calls a family council meeting after the funeral to decide how they are going to live, since there is very little money. Having inherited their father's wisdom to carry on, the children agree to take care of the house and Lillian announces that she will go to Europe to fulfill her husband's commitments. Just before the fade-out, Anne's narration informs us that Lillian Gilbreth went on to become one of the most respected psychologists in the country.

*Cheaper by the Dozen* was first-rate family entertainment. Clifton Webb, who some wags had considered "typed" in his classic Mr. Belvedere characterization, contributed a new dimension to his screen repertoire with this unforgettable portrayal of the warm and witty Frank Gilbreth. Indeed, his encounter with birth control expert Mildred Natwick supplied one of the film's funniest moments. Though overshadowed by Webb, the rest of the cast, particularly the Misses Loy and Crain, were more than equal to their tasks.

*Variety:* "Twentieth-Fox has concocted a wonderful family comedy from that novel about the very human Gilbreth tribe. . . . Trotti, as producer-scripter, hasn't attempted to film a smoothly connected story. Instead, the script hits the high-spots of a span of years and the episodes flash across the screen, leaving resounding laughter in their wake, as the picture works up to a conclusion that has a tear."

This colorful portrait of days long past was endowed with fine production values—realistically capturing the true spirit of the twenties. The public loved the film, which drew a domestic box-office gross of nearly $4.5 million.

Considering the financial success of *Cheaper by the Dozen,* it didn't take long for the powers at Fox to decide that a sequel should be made almost immediately. After all, why couldn't the Gilbreths be

***Belles on their Toes.*** **Myrna Loy and Edward Arnold.**

***Belles on their Toes.*** **Myrna Loy, Jeanne Crain, and Debra Paget.**

to the dwindling number of moviegoers of the fifties what the Hardys were to audiences of a decade earlier (i.e., a common denominator with other families, no matter where they might live).

*Belles on Their Toes* was the title of the new Technicolor project, which had Samuel G. Engel as its producer, and a primarily fictional screenplay by Phoebe and Henry Ephron. Henry Levin directed.

Opening with the graduation of the youngest Gilbreth child from college, the picture then goes into flashback—through the memories of an elderly Lillian—to a time shortly after the end of the initial film. While Mother is on her lecture tour, discussing her late husband's efficiency engineering methods, she sends her family off to Nantucket for the summer, accompanied by Tom Bracken (Hoagy Carmichael), their pugnacious houseman.[2]

2. In the original movie, this role was played by Walter Baldwin and his first name was "Jim."

But, things do not go well for Mother. Male-dominated organizations will not accept a female speaker—no matter how qualified—in place of Gilbreth, and her bookings are cancelled. Forced by finances to bring her brood back to Montclair, Lillian eventually meets Sam Harper (Edward Arnold), a self-made electric tycoon, who, after some inner struggle, asks her to train men (as she and Frank had previously done together) for his plant. Her status in the engineering world begins to climb, although there are still some areas—like the Engineer's Club of New York—that will not accept her because of her sex.

Meanwhile, Anne has met and fallen in love with Dr. Grayson (Jeffrey Hunter). She refuses his proposal of marriage, however, because, with her mother's new-found fame keeping her away from home a lot on lecture tours, she feels that she must watch over her brothers and sisters.

Learning her daughter's reason for breaking off with Bob, Lillian tells Anne that she did not raise her to be a spinster, and the young couple are reunited. On the other hand, Mother informs Harper that her life is too crowded to accept his offer of marriage.

Back in the present, Lillian gives a silent note of thanks to Frank, who gave her the inner strength to raise their fine family into adulthood.

Jeanne Crain and Myrna Loy repeated their original roles in the engaging 1952 release, as did Barbara Bates and several of the other children. Conversely, Debra Paget was a new addition to the cast, replacing Patti Brady from *Cheaper by the Dozen* as the lovely, but practical-minded, Martha.

"It was because of Debra—a good dancer—and Hoagy Carmichael," recalls director Henry Levin, "that this movie, unlike the original, was part musical. Sam Engel, the producer, figured that with this musical talent available, we might as well take advantage of it."

These tuneful interludes, featuring such pleasant, if unexceptional, songs as "Lazy," "Japanese Sandman," and "Any Rags," worked well in the handsomely produced follow-up to the 1950 hit. Again, the Gilbreth clan acted out a series of affectionate and humorous episodes with which audience members could easily find parallels in their own family life. Particularly amusing was the sequence where the Gilbreth menfolk decide that they will get rid of Al (Martin Milner), Ernestine's conceited boyfriend. While he's taking a bath, the boys parade through one-by-one, and Frank (Robert Arthur), dressed in Martha's clothes, adds the final insult to injury.

The *Hollywood Reporter*: ". . . *Belles* is sheer joy from beginning to end. . . . It is comedy with a heart."

A few critics, like the *New York Times*, bemoaned the absence of Mr. Webb in the picture: "For without the tart-tongued earthiness of Clifton Webb, this latest chapter suggests a harmless but sentimental transcription of the Old Woman in the Shoe, played with wan bravery by Myrna Loy. . . . But seasoned with sugar and everything nice, *Belles on Their Toes* is acutely needful of Mr. Webb's spicing."

Though the picture did do well financially, another sequel was out of the question. With the entire Gilbreth family grown into adulthood, what would that story have been about?

## FILMOGRAPHY

1950: *Cheaper by the Dozen* (Fox/Walter Lang) Clifton Webb.
1952: *Belles on Their Toes* (Fox/Henry Levin) Myrna Loy.

# 11 | *King Solomon's Mines*

Metro-Goldwyn-Mayer took its cast and crew to Equatorial Africa for the filming of its 1950 epic, *King Solomon's Mines*[1]—the first such location jaunt by a Hollywood company since that same studio made *Trader Horn* in 1930.

A year of elaborate preparation had preceded the production's October 17, 1949 start date in Nairobi. Indeed, it was necessary to ship 60,365 pounds of equipment to Mombasa on the African East Coast. The outfit included seven specially constructed trucks and a snow plow for use in assisting the troupe on 17,000-foot-high Mt. Kenya. Fifty-one cases, weighing a total of 9,958 pounds, carried elaborate camera and sound equipment, wardrobe, makeup, guns, tools, and props. Film was flown to Africa and back to Hollywood in custom designed, refrigerated cans that kept the Technicolor stock at a fifty-degree temperature. Reicing stations were set up in New York, the Azores, Dakar, Leopoldville, and Johannesburg on the route to Nairobi.

Starring in Helen Deutsch's screen adaptation of H. Rider Haggard's high-adventure novel was British leading man Stewart Granger as safari guide Allan Quartermain; Deborah Kerr as Elizabeth Curtis, the lady who hires the soldier-of-fortune to find her missing explorer husband; and Richard Carlson as her brother, John Goode. Initially signed by producer Sam Zimbalist to direct the film was Compton Bennett. Sequences were shot near Nairobi and Meru in Kenya, at Murchison Falls on the Victoria-Nile River in Uganda, at Stanleyville, and with the giant Watusi natives in Ruanda in the Belgian Congo.

Production proceeded anything but smoothly. Not only did the health of the cast and crew fall victim to the various African elements, but after viewing the first few weeks of rushes back in Hollywood, the powers at Metro realized that director Bennett was not delivering the exciting footage that they'd hoped for. Richard Carlson recalls the problem: "Compton Bennett was not the right director for an action film. He was a 'drawing-room' director. Also, he and Granger didn't get along at all.

"We were lucky to have Andrew Marton directing the second unit over in Africa because, if it hadn't been for him, the film would never have been finished. He was responsible for getting all the sensational action footage in the picture.

"When we returned to the studio to finish the movie, Marton took over the direction altogether."

Set near the end of the last century, the story of *King Solomon's Mines* tells how Quartermain reluctantly leads Mrs. Curtis and Goode on an expedition to locate her long-lost husband, who'd journeyed to the Dark Continent in search of the legendary mines of King Solomon. Many narrow escapes await the trio of adventurers—pythons, prowling tigers, a rampaging rhinoceros, vicious crocodiles, and, most thrilling, a terror-stricken stampede of African wildlife, madly fleeing a brush fire. Along the way, a mysterious seven-foot-tall African joins the safari and they also come across a tribe ruled by a fugitive murderer (Hugo Haas). The band escapes, killing the criminal in the process.

Following a near-lethal trek across an uncharted desert, the group reaches the land of the Watusi—a tribe of seven-foot natives, of which their mysterious African companion is the actual ruler.

Quartermain, Mrs. Curtis, and Goode are told

---

1. A British version of the story had been produced in 1937 starring Cedric Hardwicke.

***King Solomon's Mines.*** **Siriaque, Deborah Kerr, Richard Carlson, and Stewart Granger.**

***King Solomon's Mines.*** **Richard Carlson, Deborah Kerr, and Stewart Granger.**

that the lady's husband had visited this tribe months before. An evil witch doctor leads the three Britishers to the mountain cave where Curtis was last seen, then traps them there—losing his own life in the process. The cavern is the fabled hiding place of the mines of Solomon, yet lying among the riches is the skeleton of Mrs. Curtis's husband.

The trio escapes their natural prison via an underground river, but they are unable to bring any jewels along with them. After their Watusi friend kills the spurious king who'd stolen his throne, Quartermain and company are escorted back to civilization, where the explorer plans to marry the now-unattached Mrs. Curtis.

*King Solomon's Mines* was a big box-office picture (over five million dollars domestic), but critical reviews were mixed. The actors fared well in the notices and virtually all papers had nothing but praise for the film's photography and action sequences. *Variety:* "What makes this a socko piece of escapist entertainment is the authenticity it gains by being filmed on the actual locale. The camera brings Africa to life in the breath-taking beauty of color, certainly the best lensing yet of the Dark Continent. . . . The setting is alive with beauty and menace and Zimbalist's guidance of the superior cutting keeps it teeming with dangerous excitement actually far beyond the true worth of the plot."

Less impressive was indeed the script—positively juvenile in some spots, and rather dull in others. The *New York Times* summed the whole project up quite nicely when it said: "There is more than a trace of outright hokum in this thriller . . . but there is also an ample abundance of scenic novelty and beauty to compensate."

*Question:* What does a studio do with a mound of leftover African location footage?

*Answer:* They wait about ten years, then make another movie of the same type—for much less money than the first.

Such was the case with *Watusi*, a 1959 Metro release, which might properly be tagged *Son of King Solomon's Mines*. Produced by Al Zimbalist (a first cousin to Sam Zimbalist), whose other credits include such titles as *Young Dillinger* and *Cat-Women of the Moon*, this "mighty" African adventure told the story of Harry Quartermain (George Montgomery), offspring of Mr. Granger and Miss Kerr, who returns to the site of the earlier film in order to retrace the steps of his parents in quest of the legend-

**King Solomon's Mines. Richard Carlson, Deborah Kerr, and Stewart Granger.**

ary treasure. The year is 1919 and the audience learns quickly that both Harry's father and mother are dead, the latter having perished with his young sister in a U-boat attack during the Great War. Because of this tragedy, Harry has a hatred of all Germans.

Enlisting the aid of Rick Cobb (David Farrar), an old friend of his father's, Quartermain begins his journey into the jungle. Shortly, the men rescue Erica Nevler (Taina Elg), daughter of a German missionary who has been massacred by natives. Harry gives her the cold-shoulder until she cures him from a jungle fever, at which time he realizes that he loves the girl.

After many adventures, the group arrives in the land of the Watusi and are informed by the friendly natives, who fondly remember *Allan* Quartermain, that the only access to the mines is across a rock that bridges a volcanic pit. The explorers overcome the danger, rescue much of the treasure, then successfully leap the fire pit again. Realizing there are more important things in life than money, Harry decides to remain with Erica in the Watusi village, while Rick returns to civilization.

*Watusi* was filmed in fifteen days at a budget of four hundred twenty-five thousand dollars. Recalls producer Zimbalist: "We never left Los Angeles. Most of the picture was shot on the backlot."

Zimbalist took considerable unused stock footage, filmed a decade earlier in Africa, as well as some scenes intact from *King Solomon's Mines* itself, and matched them fairly well with his new backlot material to create a motion picture which, to the

untrained eye, appeared to have a quite authentic atmosphere—with thrills that equaled those in the 1950 movie. However, the astute viewer easily recognized many of these sequences from the Granger/Kerr starrer. Among the more obvious were repeats of the animal stampede and the Watusi ceremonial dance scene. Veritably, in some instances, it appeared that the producer tried to disguise the origin of the footage by inserting an optical effect or, simply, reversing a previously used shot.

James Clavell wrote the poorly conceived screenplay for this Technicolor film and Kurt Neumann was credited as director. Early in preproduction, MGM contract star Robert Taylor was suggested by the studio as possibly headlining the cast, but Zimbalist decided that George Montgomery had a better following for this low-budget type of adventure film.

Again the critics praised the original action footage from *King Solomon's Mines*. On the other hand, there were few kind words for the acting, direction, or script. The *Hollywood Reporter:* "Production by Al Zimbalist lacks the sock of his *Baby Face Nelson* and direction by Kurt Neumann lacks the power and finesse shown in his handling of *The Fly*. This may be because Clavell's script, in its constant striving to make use of stock shots, never was able to get far away from the plot patterns of an oldtime silent serial."

When Metro remade *Trader Horn* in 1973—*again* on the backlot—the producers decided that, to give the picture authenticity, it too would use stock footage from *King Solomon's Mines*. After all, who would know the difference?

Certainly not the audience.


# FILMOGRAPHY

1950: *King Solomon's Mines* (MGM/Compton Bennett, Andrew Marton) Stewart Granger.
1959: *Watusi* (MGM/Kurt Neumann) George Montgomery.

*Watusi.* **George Montgomery, Taina Elg, and David Farrar.**

*Watusi.* **George Montgomery, David Farrar, and Taina Elg.**

# 12 *The Robe*

"Did you ever hear a story about what became of the robe the soldiers gambled for at the cross?"

That provocative question, asked of famed clergyman/novelist Lloyd C. Douglas in a fan letter (penned by an Ohio housewife), was the genesis for the author's most renowned work—*The Robe*—first published in 1942. A tale about the man who crucified Christ, the inspirational book, which involved two years of research and writing, became an immediate best-seller and is, today, considered by many critics to be one of the finest novels to emerge during the past fifty years.

Producer Frank Ross, whose previous credits included *The Devil and Miss Jones* (1941), first heard of the book while chatting one Sunday afternoon with neighbor Richard Halliday, Douglas's literary agent. Although, at that time, the manuscript was only half finished and a year away from publication, Ross insisted on reading it. The producer recalled later: "I read half a story, but I felt it was one of the greatest stories of all time. I paid $100,000 for the screen rights to it, and from then on I was in frequent consultation with Douglas while he wrote the rest of the book."

In 1943, Ross made a deal with RKO to produce *The Robe* at that studio, then began developing his movie for a projected start date of not later than May 15, 1948. Set to star in the film was Gregory Peck, with Victor Fleming to direct. But, prior to the 1948 deadline, billionaire Howard Hughes acquired the controlling interest in RKO and, though more than seven hundred-fifty thousand dollars had thus far been spent to prepare the epic, its production was cancelled. The wealthy eccentric, it seems, was not interested in making religious pictures . . . especially ones budgeted at over five million dollars.

Rights to the property were tied up in litigation until 1952, when Ross convinced Darryl F. Zanuck at Fox that he should buy out RKO's interest in the best-seller and do the filmization at his Pico Boulevard lot—starring Tyrone Power.

Scaling down the production's budget to $3.5 million (it later climbed back to $4.5), Ross set to work again. Gina Kaus had previously done the adaptation of Douglas's novel, and, now, Philip Dunne was called in to execute a final screenplay. Signed to direct the Fox production was Henry Koster.

Principal photography was scheduled to begin during the fall of 1952 and, in preparation, construction was begun on the film's half-million dollars worth of sets. However, when this new production start date rolled around, there was another delay, but, this time, Ross was more than happy to postpone his cameras until late January of 1953.

Constantly trying to find new gimmicks that would pull audiences away from their television sets and back into the movie houses, Fox had acquired the exclusive rights to a new French wide-screen process—ultimately dubbed CinemaScope[1]—and wanted *The Robe* to be the first picture that made use of the procedure. It was going to take a few months to perfect the system, as well as adapt the studio's existing cameras for its use. Hence, the delay.

When the cameras finally did begin to roll on the sixty-day shooting schedule—over ten years after Frank Ross had acquired the novel from Douglas, who had died in 1951—it was with a brand new,

1. Unlike Cinerama, which relied on three projectors to achieve its effect, the Fox process utilized only one projector and one strip of 35mm film.

*The Robe.* Jean Simmons and Richard Burton.

*The Robe.* Victor Mature and Richard Burton.

**The Robe.** Richard Burton and Michael Rennie.

**The Robe.** Jay Robinson and Jean Simmons.

albeit talented, cast: Richard Burton, Jean Simmons, Victor Mature, Michael Rennie, Jay Robinson, Dean Jagger, Richard Boone, and in one of his first screen roles, an effective one-scene cameo by Michael Ansara as Judas.

Running 135 minutes, *The Robe* tells of Roman Tribune Marcellus Gallio (Burton), his proud Greek slave, Demetrius (Mature), and childhood sweetheart Diana (Simmons), whose guardian wishes her to marry the vicious heir to the throne, Caligula (Robinson).

The Tribune is assigned to a new post in Jerusalem and there encounters a man riding on a donkey, whom crowds hail as the Messiah. Although Marcellus is contemptuous of this "troublemaker," Demetrius is truly moved and becomes one of his followers.

Prior to his return to Rome, Marcellus is given the routine task of executing "three criminals"—one

of which is Jesus. In the shadow of the cross, the officer gambles for and wins the homespun robe of the prophet and, after throwing the cloth across his shoulders to protect himself from a sudden storm, becomes a stricken man—sick with the guilt of his murderous act. Demetrius, in turn, seizes the robe and strides off—to freedom.

Back in Rome, Emperor Tiberius (Ernest Thesiger) orders the Tribune to find and destroy the robe, in order to restore his sanity, and to ferret out the "treasonous" follows of Christ.

His travels in Jerusalem bring Marcellus into contact with the disciples of Jesus—Justus (Jagger), Miriam (Betta St. John), and Peter (Rennie), the "Big Fisherman." But it is his ultimate confrontation with Demetrius, guardian of the robe, that converts the Roman to Christianity.

Meanwhile, Caligula has become emperor and orders his soldiers to stop the new radical religious movement that threatens the status quo. Marcellus, successful in rescuing a captured Demetrius from the royal torture chamber, is himself apprehended and brought before the mad ruler for trial. Whereas the Tribune reaffirms his allegiance to Rome and his emperor, he refuses to deny his belief in Christ and, therefore, signs his own death warrant. Rather than live without him, Diana chooses to die with Marcellus. The couple march off—realizing they will be together in a better world.

*The Robe,* released in 1953, was a tremendous box-office hit ($17.5 million domestic gross), owing its success to the combination of a presold story that the public wanted to see and the novelty of Cinema-Scope. Reviews, however, were mixed. *Variety:* "Koster rates credit for his directorial work in bringing *The Robe* to the screen. He moved his people and scenes extremely well and got top-grade performances from the entire cast."

Critics of the production insisted—and rightly so—that much of the intimacy and sensitivity of Douglas' work was lost in the exciting new wide-screen wonder. The *New York Times* called Ross' film: ". . . a historical drama less compelling than the process by which it is shown . . . essentially a smashing display of spectacle.

". . . an unwavering force of personal drama is missed in the size and the length of the show, and a full sense of spiritual experience is lost in the physicalness of the display."

"It begins where *The Robe* left off" is the way Fox heralded *Demetrius and the Gladiators* (working titles: *The Gladiators* and *The Story of Demetrius*).

The idea of doing a sequel to *The Robe* had not occurred to Frank Ross until the final four month postponement of the parent film in October of 1952, to await the practical development of CinemaScope. "Years ago," the producer recalled in 1954, "I felt that the full magnificence of the story of *The Robe* would require two feature-length pictures. But as work continued on the story, I saw the job could be

*Demetrius and the Gladiators.* **Victor Mature and Michael Rennie.**

*Demetrius and the Gladiators.* **Susan Hayward and Ernest Borgnine.**

done with a single production and abandoned the idea. After that, I had too much trouble bringing *The Robe* to production to be worrying about a sequel. But we were all set to go when Mr. Zanuck decided to wait for CinemaScope, and for the first time in ten years, I had a chance to sit back and relax.

"In the script of *The Robe*, we had left Demetrius a fugitive Christian in pagan Rome, which, of course, implied a future of great excitement for him."

Working again with writer Philip Dunne (and with Darryl Zanuck's blessing), Ross decided that since *The Robe* was essentially the tale of the acquisition of faith, *Demetrius and the Gladiators* should concern itself with the trial of the faith acquired.

This ninety-nine-minute/$3.5 million production, shot on the same sets as the first movie (the only new construction of any consequence was Caligula's arena), was directed by Delmer Daves, who reflects: "*The Robe* was still filming when I began shooting *Demetrius*. My picture was scheduled so that, as the first film finished with a particular set or an actor [Mature, who'd achieved the finest performance of his career in *The Robe*, Rennie, and Jay Robinson were the only artists appearing in both productions], I was then able to make use of them. In fact, since *The Robe* began shooting without a Caligula, I wound up directing the tests for that role, primarily

*Demetrius and the Gladiators.* Anne Bancroft, Victor Mature, and William Marshall.

*Demetrius and the Gladiators.* Barry Jones, Jay Robinson, and Victor Mature.

because the part was much larger in the second movie."

Beginning with the final scene of *The Robe* where Marcellus and Diana are led off to be executed, Dunne's original plot, in short order, has Demetrius being arrested—for beating a Roman soldier who was searching for the robe (Caligula, believing it has magic powers, has ordered the garment brought to him)—and sentenced to be trained as a gladiator in a school owned by Claudius (Barry Jones), aged uncle to Caligula, and his young, unfaithful wife, Messalina (Susan Hayward).

In his first arena action, Demetrius wins, but, because he is a Christian, refuses the emperor's order to kill his opponent, Glycon (William Marshall). Caligula orders the Greek's throat cut. Messalina, however, is attracted to the handsome slave and intercedes, suggesting it would be more diverting to watch Demetrius fight three tigers. The contest between man and beast is a furious one, but Demetrius, though wounded, emerges victorious.

When Lucia (Debra Paget), the young girl who Demetrius loves, apparently dies at the hands of five of his fellow gladiators, the Greek renounces his faith and, the next day, slays the quintet in the arena. So spectacular is his win that Caligula grants him his freedom, appointing him Tribune in the Praetorian Guard. The ex-slave also begins a torrid affair with Messalina.

Brought back to his senses by a visit from the Apostle Peter, Demetrius breaks off with the shrewd woman. Later, when the emperor orders him to bring in the robe, he goes to the Big Fisherman and asks him to surrender the garment to save the lives of thousands of Christians. Peter shows his former follower that the robe is held tightly in the grip of Lucia, who is not dead, but only in a trance. Demetrius' prayers to his God for the restoration of the girl's health are answered.

When the Greek brings Caligula the robe, the insane ruler has a prisoner in the dungeon slain in order to test the holy cloth's magic powers. The experiment fails, thereby enraging the emperor. Horrified at what Caligula has done, Demetrius lunges at the sovereign and, as punishment, is ordered back to the arena to meet the dread Marco (Karl Davis), Caligula's bodyguard. The Christian refuses to do combat. Unwilling to permit the death of their hero and disenchanted with the emperor's tyrannical ways, the Praetorian Guard spears Marco before he can murder Demetrius and, after him, Caligula.

Assuming the throne, Claudius states that he has feigned weakness because any evidence of strength would have cost his life. Messalina renounces her past acts and promises to perform her proper functions as wife to the emperor. The new ruler forgives Demetrius and tells him that, as long as Christians are not disloyal to the state, they will not be molested.

Whereas The Robe was more of a thoughtful religious drama, Demetrius and the Gladiators put its emphasis on the action. Performances, as in the original, were fine and Daves's direction kept the story moving at a fast tempo. Yet this new film, also endowed with the new wide-screen process and Technicolor, seemed to lack the meticulous care that had been so apparent in its predecessor. How, indeed, could a picture, hastily conceived and rushed in its preparation to meet a previously determined (for budgetary purposes)[2] start date, hope to have the same well-planned story values and development that had taken ten years to accomplish in its parent production? Veritably, with all its spectacle and exciting action sequences, what Demetrius really lacked—on a comparative basis—was "class."

The New York Times called the 1954 release "a good old-fashioned Roman circus film. . . . This one is no more like The Robe than either of them is like nature or Roman history."

Despite its shortcomings, Demetrius did entertain audiences and, though not achieving the same high quality or grosses ($4.25 million domestic) as the original, certainly was an honorable attempt to create a viable sequel to what is generally regarded as a minor classic in the religious/spectacle film genre.

## FILMOGRAPHY

1953: *Robe, The* (Fox/Henry Koster) Richard Burton.
1954: *Demetrius and the Gladiators* (Fox/Delmer Daves) Victor Mature.

2. Considerable money was saved by shooting both films at the same time.

# 13    *Creature from the Black Lagoon*

The 1950s brought about a change in movie monsters. No longer did these night stalkers spring from the demented brains of misguided scientists or from European folktales come to life. Instead, we now had uncanny visitors from outer space, gigantic beasts resulting from the atomic bomb, or "missing links" resurrected by meddling explorers. The classic example of this latter category and possibly the most original monster to emerge from this era, was Universal's Gill Man—the *Creature from the Black Lagoon* (1954).

As they were with the horror fare of the thirties and forties, Universal had quickly become the acknowledged leader of science-fiction entertainment—their most successful practitioner of this genre being house producer William Alland, a graduate of Orson Welles's Mercury Theatre, whose film credits include everything from *It Came from Outer Space* (1953) and *Tarantula* (1955) to *Chief Crazy Horse* (1955) with Victor Mature.

The idea for the Gill Man came to Alland as the result of an evening out with Orson Welles, Dolores Del Rio, and a Mexican cameraman named Figueroa. Recalls the producer: "Over dinner, Figueroa told us about these legendary fish creatures of the Amazon, who come out of the water and attack people. I didn't really believe the story, but I knew that there might be the basis of a new monster film here."

The studio also liked the premise of the man/fish and writer Maurice Zimm was set to develop a story line. Although Zimm's plot contained many elements that were retained in the final picture, Alland felt that certain basic changes were necessary. Hence, another writer, Arthur Ross, was engaged to do the screenplay.

Arthur Ross: "As I recall, the original story dealt with a mad scientist in the Amazon region who comes across this *upright* 'half-thing/half-man' and uses it to achieve his own devious ends. The plot was much like the old *Frankenstein* films.

"Cousteau's *Silent World* had recently been published and I thought it might be better to make the scientists heroes, instead of villains. I also planned a lot of underwater sequences and indicated to Alland that one terrifying aspect that could be utilized in the picture—aside from the monster—was man's basic fear of drowning.

"My quasiscientific basis for the creature was inspired by a story I'd read years before, Homer Smith's 'Kamongo,' which told of the lung fish, an unusual species that lives in Africa. I felt that the Gill Man could be another such 'dead end of nature.'

"Actually, I only wrote the first draft of the screenplay. Alland liked it, but thought that there should be more of the 'beauty and the beast' element in the film—the monster should be attracted to the girl. I didn't agree, going by the philosophy that 'a fish is a fish is a fish.' Therefore, Harry Essex was called in to rewrite my script to include a 'love story.'"

While the screenplay was being written, Alland hired a Russian sculptor to create his title character. Alland: "What he designed was a rather haunting, sensitive, almost handsome, monster. Unfortunately, the studio wanted the creature to look much scarier, so Bud Westmore was asked to modify the makeup."

*Creature from the Black Lagoon* (Original title: *Black Lagoon*) tells of a group of scientists, who, after the discovery of a web-fingered skeleton hand in the Amazon region, head into the uncharted tropics to hunt the remainder of the fossil. Members of the expedition include: David Reed (Richard

*Creature from the Black Lagoon.* **Julie Adams and the Gill Man.**

Carlson), hero of the story; Kay Lawrence (Julia Adams), his fiancée and object of the Gill Man's (Ben Chapman) affections; Lucas (Nestor Paiva), captain of the riverboat the group has chartered; and publicity-seeking Mark Williams (Richard Denning), who, when he finally sees the living creature that has killed several secondary members of his party, is determined to bring it back to civilization.

The Gill Man is captured once, but escapes—nearly killing another scientist (Whit Bissell) at the time. Over Williams's objections, the other explorers, led by Reed, decide to depart the inlet to seek help, but the monster has blocked the lagoon, desiring revenge for the attack upon himself and having designs on Kay. In the final minutes of the film, it kills Williams by dragging the struggling opportunist down to the murky depths of his jungle pool, then kidnaps the heroine. Reed and his companions track the creature to a hidden cave, where Kay is rescued and the Gill Man "fatally" wounded by rifle fire.

Under the direction of Jack Arnold, *Creature* was shot in 3-D black and white on location in Florida, as well as on the massive Universal backlot. Budget was four hundred-fifty thousand dollars. Superb underwater sequences, featuring aqua-lung equipped divers chasing the monster, were directed by James C. Havens. According to producer Alland: "This was the first Hollywood picture to utilize 'free swimming' underwater sequences. Prior to this, all such filming was done in tanks, either on sound stages or

backlots. But, thanks to a new camera developed by Charles 'Scotty' Welbourne, we were able to shoot our scenes in a natural lake."

Critical reaction to the picture was mixed. *Variety* called it: ". . . a well-made horror feature guaranteed to spook the chiller fan and amuse others. It has excellent exploitation possibilities."

On the other hand, the *New York Times* commented: "It's a fishing expedition that is necessary only if a viewer has lost all of his comic books."

Nevertheless, the sometimes leisurely paced production did supply enough thrills to please its audiences and, most importantly, garnered an impressive box office. Based on these figures, Universal executives decided that the Gill Man had only been stunned by the barrage of bullets fired at him, since a sequel was definitely in order.

3-D was on its way out when *Revenge of the Creature* debuted in theaters in March of 1955, prompting Universal to give exhibitors a choice as to whether they would play this three hundred-fifty-thousand-dollar follow-up with the gimmicky process or in ordinary photography. Alland, again, produced and Jack Arnold reprised as director, but a new writer, Martin Berkeley, did the uninspired screenplay, based on Alland's story.

Joe Hayes (John Bromfield), with the aid of the blowsy South American riverman, Lucas (Paiva—

80

*Creature from the Black Lagoon.* **Nestor Paiva, Julie Adams, Richard Carlson, and Antonio Moreno.**

Producer William Alland, assigned three hundred-fifty thousand dollars as his budget, talked writer Arthur Ross into returning to the fold for this one, having been unable to secure his services for the previous year's excursion into the world of weird fish. Ross, who, this time, received sole credit for both a story and screenplay, which he wrote within a four-week period, reflects: "Alland wasn't that happy with the second *Creature* picture, so he asked me to come up with an idea for the third that would have a stronger science-fiction quality—like we had with the original.

"I decided to enlarge on an idea that had been suggested in the first picture. That is, to explore the

the only holdover from the original picture), manages to capture the Gill Man (played by several divers this time) and brings him from his Amazon environment to the Marine Gardens in Florida, where scientists Clete Ferguson (John Agar) and Helen Dobson (Lori Nelson) plan to determine the creature's mental capacity. Within three weeks, the lady has taught the Gill Man the meaning of the word "Stop!," while, at the same time, he has become smitten with her.

Escaping from the tank that holds him prisoner, the monster kills Hayes, overturns an automobile, then disappears into the Florida waters, later emerging from time to time to frighten the populace. He abducts Helen from the arms of Ferguson, while the two are together at a seafood restaurant. A chase ensues, with the hero advising the local police on how to handle the situation. When the beast is finally cornered, Ferguson yells "Stop!" and Gill Man obeys long enough for Helen to escape—before the authorities begin firing away.

*Hollywood Reporter:* "The result is something that seems best described as 'complacent horror' for, although all the routine motions have been made to please that portion of the public that delights in seeing a man in a rubber forehead carrying a girl in a crepe de Chine through an underlighted corridor toward an undetermined end, it has none of that superlative bogey-man craftsmanship which made *Frankenstein, Dracula,* and *The Thing From Outer Space* such good red meat in the theatre."

More good grosses, and the Universal lords decreed that Gill Man should rise again. *The Creature Walks Among Us* (1956), directed by John Sherwood, was, like its two predecessors, shot in glorious black and white, but was without 3-D.

*Revenge of the Creature.* **The Gill Man and John Bromfield.**

question whether a particular species—in this case, the Gill Man—could be modified by his environment and/or surgery. I had my hero argue that it was his primitive environment that made the creature wild and that, if the original lung fish theory was valid, then underneath this monster was the emergent man.

"The script also played with the question: Can you diminish primeval fear in primitive animals by the creation of an environment of protection and kindness?"

Not only was *The Creature Walks Among Us* a monster movie, but it also had a secondary "eternal triangle" plot going for it.

Wealthy marine biologist Dr. William Barton (Jeff Morrow), his wife, Marcia (Leigh Snowden), Dr. Thomas Morgan (Rex Reason), and guide Jed Grant (Gregg Palmer) journey into the Florida Everglades to capture the "merman" that has, according to recent folktales, been roaming these swamplands. In a nighttime encounter with the humans, Gill Man is collared, but not before he is severely burned by the flames from a kerosene lamp.

The creature's gills have been destroyed by the fire, so, in order to save his life, the scientists perform major surgery, which turns him into a totally lung-breathing animal. Yet, his natural instincts still draw the former fish to water, unaware that—without gills—he will drown. It is quick action by Morgan that saves him from such a fate when he goes for a moonlight swim in the ocean.

The seemingly docile (from Morgan's kind treatment) ex-Gill Man is taken, via Barton's lavish yacht, to the biologist's large estate in California, where he is put in a compound, surrounded by an electrically-charged fence. In the meantime, Grant has been making advances toward Mrs. Barton, who is actually attracted to Morgan. Insanely jealous, Barton murders the guide, then attempts to pin the crime on the creature. Super fish, objecting to this frame-up, breaks out of his prison, and kills Barton, leaving Morgan and Marcia to pursue their love in earnest. We last see Gill Man on the shores of the Pacific Ocean, debating whether or not he should return to his origins. As the scene fades out, he moves off in the direction of the water.

Astute viewers of this finale to the series noted immediately that two different actors were interpreting the title role. Prior to the fire sequence, excellent swimmer Ricou Browning donned the

***Revenge of the Creature.* The Gill Man escapes.**

costume, but, following the operation, the larger framed Don Megowan assumed the part. William Alland explains: "After we'd completed the Florida scenes, Browning started making certain demands regarding billing and other matters. But, the studio wouldn't go along with him, so he was replaced. Where we made our mistake was that we didn't choose another actor of the same general build as Ricou to replace him. Everyone knew we'd switched actors."

Though some spectators liked this entry's dual plot structure, most critics had few words of praise for the production, preferring to take a tongue-in-cheek approach like that expressed in the *New York Times*: "The 'creature,' of course, is frightening enough to scare the scales off a tarpon. However he apparently hasn't terrified his Hollywood discoverers. Chances are he'll be back."

But, fortunately or unfortunately (depending upon your point of view), he wasn't. Mr. Alland suggests the reasons: "By the time the last film was made, television was getting very big and this picture didn't do as well as the others at the box office. Besides, I didn't want to make any more. I'd really gotten involved in the first one, but these last two were just 'spit-out.' It was time to quit while we were ahead."

If the three *Creature* pictures have failed to achieve the same immortality as Universal's earlier excursions into the macabre, Gill Man's terrifying

appearance certainly cannot be blamed. More likely, the fault lies in the fact that all of these mildly entertaining projects had little more than adequate story lines, as well as rather bland leading men and women to speak the often stilted dialogue. With the exception of Nestor Paiva's colorful riverboat captain, where in the science-fiction series can one find characters as interesting as Bela Lugosi's arch-villain, Ygor, or Lionel Atwill's mechanical armed Inspector Krogh?[1] Touches such as these would have assured the features themselves a position in the Horror Hall of Fame to rival that of the exquisitely eerie makeup of their star.

Perhaps the basic problem is best summed up by an old Bob Hope joke: "A 4-D movie? That's a 3-D movie with a plot."

## FILMOGRAPHY

1954: *Creature from the Black Lagoon* (U/Jack Arnold) Richard Carlson.

1955: *Revenge of the Creature* (U/Jack Arnold) John Agar.

1956: *Creature Walks Among Us, The* (U/John Sherwood) Jeff Morrow.

1. Both characters appear in *Son of Frankenstein.*

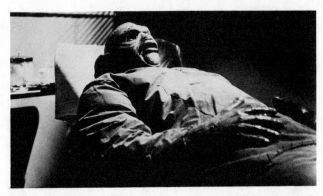

***The Creature Walks Among Us.* The altered Gill Man.**

***The Creature Walks Among Us.* Leigh Snowden and Rex Reason.**

***Revenge of the Creature.* Lori Nelson, John Agar, and the Gill Man.**

# 14    *Peyton Place*

Many people must have shaken their heads in wonderment when Jerry Wald first announced that he would transfer *Peyton Place*, Grace Metalious's sexsational runaway best-seller to the screen. Hers was a bold book, featuring a violent rape, an abortion, and several explicit scenes of fornication. Critics may not have considered the multifaceted tome "art," but the average reader loved it. Considering Hollywood's then strict Production Code, producer Wald's chosen task of adaptation did not appear to be an easy one.

With the aid of writer John Michael Hayes, Wald set to work on this story about a small New England town, in which sin and hypocrisy thrive under a respectable surface. The men quickly discovered that the elimination of the novel's offensive sequences did not really destroy either the potency or spirit of Miss Metalious's original piece. Critical scenes of a questionable nature (such as the rape of Selena Cross by her stepfather) were maintained for their dramatic values, yet altered in such a way so that they wouldn't outrage the citizenry. Characters also (like Betty Anderson, the town tramp in the book, who is paid off by the rich mill owner when she becomes pregnant by his son) underwent major transformations to make them more acceptable to the puritanical in the audience.

In an interview with *Variety*, prior to the film's release, Wald indicated how these story changes would work, by using the aforementioned abortion scene as an example: "I felt the scene was in bad taste. I personally didn't want it. I felt it was unnecessary. It's been changed in the film, so that the episode becomes a miscarriage.

"We retain the scene where the stepfather attacks his stepdaughter, and she's going to have a child, but I saw no reason for the abortion sequence as presented in the novel. There are other compensating values.

"As it is, we don't offend the innocent, and don't frustrate the intelligent, adult picturegoer."

The producer's "sex by suggestion" approach may have placated organizations like the Legion of Decency, but not the town of Woodstock, Vermont, where he'd initially planned to lens his movie. Irked because they felt their community was the model for Miss Metalious's book (her husband had once taught in the local school system), the townsfolk refused to cooperate with the film people and the production location was ultimately moved to Camden, Maine.

Directed by Mark Robson, this 1957 Twentieth Century-Fox release views the lives of several diverse, albeit intertwined, characters, who reside in Peyton Place—months before the bombing of Pearl Harbor. There is Constance MacKenzie (Lana Turner), an attractive "widow," who runs a local dress shop while strictly raising her teenage daughter, Allison (Diane Varsi); Michael Rossi (Lee Philips), the new high school principal and would-be suitor to Constance; the wise and helpful country physician, Dr. Swain (Lloyd Nolan); Selena Cross (Hope Lange), Allison's girlfriend from the "other side of the tracks," living with her weak mother, Nellie (Betty Field), drunken stepfather, Lucas (Arthur Kennedy), and young brother; Norman Page (Russ Tamblyn), the shy boy with an overbearing mother; Ted Carter (David Nelson),

84

*Peyton Place*. Diane Varsi and Lana Turner.

*Peyton Place*. Diane Varsi and Russ Tamblyn.

*Peyton Place.* **Lana Turner, Lloyd Nolan, and Lee Philips.**

*Peyton Place.* **David Nelson and Hope Lange.**

Selena's "true-blue" boyfriend; and Betty Anderson (Terry Moore), the "fast" girl, who loves and *marries* wealthy Rodney Harrington (Barry Coe), much to his father's (Leon Ames) disapproval.

Once these characters have been established,

events in the 166-minute drama move rather swiftly: Lucas Cross, in one of his drunken stupors, rapes Selena, then runs off—leaving his distraught wife, Nellie, to hang herself. Dr. Swain assists the impregnated girl with a miscarriage—vowing to remain silent about the incident. Elsewhere in Peyton Place, Allison learns that she is, in fact, illegitimate—the result of an affair her mother once had with a now-deceased married man. Unable to face Constance, the teenager, an aspiring writer, runs off to New York.

Later, with the coming of the war, all the town's young men are drafted. Norman Page steps out of character and distinguishes himself in the paratroops, but on the tragic side of the ledger, Rodney Harrington is killed in action, leaving his father and wife Betty to console each other.

With her young brother, Selena has attempted to build a life for herself in Peyton Place. However, the return of Lucas—on furlough from the Navy—shatters this. When her stepfather attempts to have his way with her again, she kills him and is arrested for murder.

The well-publicized trial of her friend brings Allison home. She, unfortunately, is unable to be of any material help in the case, but Dr. Swain is. By revealing the terrible wrong that Lucas had done to Selena, the man of medicine turns the tide of the proceedings and the girl—no longer ashamed of what was not her fault—is acquitted.

The picture ends happily, with Constance, now engaged to Rossi, reunited with her daughter and Selena walking off, hand-in-hand, with Ted Carter.

Virtually presold to the public long before the cameras began to turn, *Peyton Place*, shot in DeLuxe color and CinemaScope, was a box-office bonanza ($11.5 million domestic gross), as well as—for its genre—an exceptional motion picture. Robson accurately captured the everyday life of a small town through scenes like the high school graduation and Fourth of July picnic, and, at the same time, drew some fine performances from his cast, several of which (Misses Turner, Lange, and Varsi, and, of the men, Kennedy and Tamblyn) were Oscar nominated. Though a bit slow-moving at times, Mr. Hayes's sreenplay contained enough high points to keep viewers intrigued.

The *New York Times:* ". . . the interlocked dramas of several persons that she [Grace Metalious] pursues in her tale are put forth with strength and fascination —and comparative credibility—in this film. Except that they take a long time at it."

With the success of the movie ensured, Jerry Wald suggested to Grace Metalious that she write a sequel to her novel—and, thus was born *Return to Peyton Place*.

"No director in town wanted to touch this project," recalls Jose Ferrer. "I took the job because I wasn't that much in demand as a director then and needed the credit.

"Five scripts for *Return to Peyton Place* had been written before I entered the picture and none of them worked. So, at my agent's suggestion, I got Jerry Wald to hire Ronald Alexander, a writer who seemed to have the answers to the story problems.

"In this sequel, we decided to do *Peyton Place* in New York, rather than in Peyton Place, since *Peyton Place* had been done in the original."

A few months after the release of the first picture, Diane Varsi, a Fox contract player, had become disenchanted with the Hollywood scene and departed. Therefore, when it came time to make the 1961 follow-up, she was unavailable to repeat her role of Allison, as was Lana Turner in the part of Connie.

Rather than cause confusion by mixing old and new players in the established roles from the last film, Wald decided to recast entirely. Eleanor Parker was set (after Gene Tierney proved unavailable) to take over from Miss Turner in the role of Connie,

*Return to Peyton Place.* **Jeff Chandler and Carol Lynley.**

*Return to Peyton Place.* **Luciana Paluzzi and Brett Halsey.**

now the wife of Mike Rossi—an assignment assumed by Robert Sterling. Carol Lynley was Allison, Tuesday Weld played Selena, and Brett Halsey essayed David Nelson's part of Ted Carter. None of the other set characters appeared in the sequel, although, in one of the early screenplays, Dr. Swain had been included, but was later eliminated when it was decided his presence served no purpose. Yet, the most interesting role in this new production was that of Roberta Carter, Ted's rich and possessive mother—originally offered to Joan Crawford, then Bette Davis, but finally played by Mary Astor.

Also filmed in CinemaScope and DeLuxe color, the new Fox production contradicted several events that had occurred in its predecessor. Most obvious was the fact that the time element had been moved forward. Whereas *Peyton Place* had concluded during the mid-forties, this new film—ostensibly taking

*Return to Peyton Place.* **Eleanor Parker, Carol Lynley, and Mary Astor.**

place a year or so later—was set in the present (1961). Characters, too, had undergone transformations. The Selena Cross of Miss Weld was a much harder person than Hope Lange had played her, and, even more surprising, Carol Lynley's Allison had regressed from when we last saw her in the person of Diane Varsi, who had developed the part into a mature young woman. This new Allison seemed little more than a silly teenager and, indeed, no mention was ever made of the fact that, in the earlier picture, she'd lived in New York for a number of months.

Three basic story lines developed simultaneously in *Return to Peyton Place:* (1) Allison writes a novel based on the events in the first movie, journeys to New York alone (for the *first?* time), and, while developing and promoting the book into a best-seller, falls in love with her married publisher, Lewis Jackman (Jeff Chandler); (2) Selena Cross, emotionally and socially troubled by the events in her past, is helped by Allison's new exposé of a fictional Peyton Place, which points the town's residents out as a

bunch of hypocrites. There is also a new romance for Selena—a ski-instructor (Gunnar Hellstrom); (3) Roberta Carter, unsuccessful in her attempts to destroy son Ted's marriage to Raffaella (Luciana Paluzzi), a girl he'd met while at law school, later tries to have Mike Rossi fired as principal when he refuses to remove Allison's biting new book from the school library.

The climactic scene occurs at an old-fashioned New England-style town meeting, when all the principal characters—including her son—stand against Roberta on the matter of the scandalous volume, and Rossi is reinstated.

The next day, Allison and Jackman part, realizing their relationship has no future. Presumably, everybody else lives happily ever after.

Originally, producer Wald had planned a much more dramatic conclusion for his picture: Following her shattering defeat at the town meeting, Mrs. Carter returns home where her mental condition deteriorates rapidly. She subsequently dies in a fire, accidentally ignited, from which her son is unable to rescue her.

Though these scenes were shot, it was later decided that—with the movie already running a *slow*

123 minutes—it was best to eliminate them in favor of the more psychological climax at the meeting.

*Return to Peyton Place* may not have touched the box-office grosses of its parent film, but the financial returns it did garner ($4.5 million domestic) were nothing to be ashamed about.

From the standpoint of aesthetics, however, the picture was, in all areas, a far cry from the quality of *Peyton Place*. Hampered with a story line that did little more than rehash the events of the 1957 release, Ferrer was unable to generate much life into the proceedings and, with the exception of Miss Astor's chilling portrait of the matron who gradually loses her control over the people in the town, brought forth merely competent performances from his cast. In all fairness, however, even the finest actors and directors would have had a difficult time making such bland basic material work.

The *Hollywood Reporter:* "The first *Peyton Place* was a superior film based on a mediocre novel. The second *Peyton Place* does not rise above its source material."

As usual, the *New York Times* had its comments: "*Return to Peyton Place* . . . is more a take-out of a mean and selfish mother than it is a sequel to the film *Peyton Place.* . . . Let's say the script of Ronald Alexander is simply shallow and diffuse, and the direction of Jose Ferrer does very little to improve on these qualities."

Miss Metalious's novel, of course, later became the basis of television's first prime-time soap opera, introducing to the public such young talents as Mia Farrow, Ryan O'Neal, Barbara Parkins, and Leigh Taylor-Young. After the demise of this popular show, the material was utilized to spawn a daytime soaper.

Its title may still carry a wicked connotation, but, by today's standards, the once-shocking novel entitled *Peyton Place* is actually quite tame. Veritably, if the moral structure in our society becomes any more permissive than it is already, it wouldn't be too surprising if a cartoon version of the piece showed up someday for the kiddies on Saturday morning television.

## FILMOGRAPHY

1957: *Peyton Place* (Fox/Mark Robson) Lana Turner.
1961: *Return to Peyton Place* (Fox/Jose Ferrer) Carol Lynley.

**Return to Peyton Place. Tuesday Weld and Gunnar Hellstrom.**

# 15  *Gunfight at the O.K. Corral*

On October 26, 1881 in Tombstone, Arizona, U.S. Marshal Wyatt Earp, his brothers, Virgil and Morgan, and alcoholic dentist-turned-gambler/gun-slinger Doc Holliday met the notorious Clanton and McLowery clans at the O.K. Corral to partake in the most infamous face-to-face shootout in the history of the West. Within thirty seconds of the first shot being fired, Tom and Frank McLowery were dead, and young Billy Clanton lay bleeding in the street—his demise less than a half-hour away. Aside from a shoulder wound sustained by Morgan, the Earp camp was virtually untouched in the battle.

The long-running Earp/Clanton feud was by no means ended, but this short, violent incident quickly became legend—with less than accurate chroniclers writing of how the noble Earp faction[1] vanquished the dastardly villains, making things safe again for "honest folk" in wicked Tombstone. In the near century that has passed since that bloody day, the showdown at the O.K. Corral has become symbolic of the romantic West (i.e., the folktales that excite us in our youth and whose truth we prefer to the real historical facts).

Hollywood has told of the relationship between Earp and Holliday and their fateful confrontation with the Clantons and McLowerys on numerous occasions. John Ford's total fictionalization (Holliday was killed in the battle) was entitled *My Darling Clementine* (1946) and featured Henry Fonda as Earp and Victor Mature as the former dentist. Most recently, Stacy Keach was John "Doc" Holliday and Harris Yulin the lawman in director Frank Perry's *Doc* (1971).

Certainly the most popular ($4.7 million domestic gross) version of the saga was *Gunfight at the O.K. Corral*, produced in 1957 by Hal B. Wallis for Paramount. Packed with excitement, the Technicolor/VistaVision release was somewhat of a departure from the more cerebral, adult-themed westerns like *The Gunfighter* (1950), *High Noon* (1952), and *Shane* (1953), which had been playing movie houses since the beginning of the decade. True, the well-constructed screenplay by Leon Uris did develop the compassionate friendship of mutual respect and dignity between Earp (Burt Lancaster) and Holliday (Kirk Douglas) more fully than any previous film on the subject and the two *then*-top box-office stars brought these characters colorfully to life. Yet, the emphasis in this production was the *action*, and that's what ultimately brought the patrons into the theaters.

Uris's script begins in Fort Griffin, Texas, with the two heroes meeting when the peace officer saves Holliday from a lynch mob. The jaded gunman follows his benefactor to Dodge City, Kansas, where he returns the favor by helping Earp out of a difficult situation with some rowdy cowboys. After that, the oddly assorted pair become constant companions and, when Wyatt moves on to Tombstone to help his brothers get rid of the Clantons, Holliday tags along. From that point, the picture builds quickly, climaxing, of course, with the showdown at the O.K. Corral.

Smartly directed by John Sturges, *Gunfight at the O.K. Corral* alluded to many actual events in the lives of Earp and Holliday, but the detailed handling of these situations was primarily fiction. The final shootout, for instance, was greatly embellished in this filming to delight the action-craving audiences.

1. More honest researchers have revealed that Marshal Wyatt Earp was certainly susceptible to a bribe and was even known to have operated a Tombstone brothel.

During the *real* gunfight, only three of the outlaws had perished; however, in the Paramount production, the entire Clanton/McLowery gangs,[2] as well as Johnny Ringo (John Ireland), who had nothing at all to do with the incident, were slain by Lancaster, Douglas, and company.

Also created especially for this version was the character of Laura Denbow (Rhonda Fleming), a lady gambler, who supplied the upstanding marshal with occasional romance.

Even with these and other regular departures from the truth, most critics were impressed with the movie. The *Hollywood Reporter* said: "Hal Wallis' *Gunfight at the O.K. Corral* is certainly the best western of the year and to say this is to say the least you can about this terrific Paramount production. . . . The excitement kindles in the opening frames and is relentless throughout."

Taking a more conservative viewpoint, the *New York Times* commented: "*Gunfight at the O.K. Corral* is not *High Noon*."

2. Lyle Bettger headed the "baddies" as Ike Clanton and Dennis Hopper was his brother, Billy.

*Gunfight at the O.K. Corral.* **The Clantons and the Earps meet for the final showdown.**

*Gunfight at the O.K. Corral.* **Burt Lancaster and Kirk Douglas.**

John Sturges's involvement with the Earps, Doc Holliday, and the Clantons did not end when he banked his final paycheck for the Lancaster/Douglas starrer. A decade later, he became intrigued with another project about these historical characters and proceeded to prepare what would become *Hour of the Gun* (1967), a "sequel" to his earlier film.

"I don't like to call *Hour of the Gun* a sequel," states the director. "It was conceived independently from Wallis's picture; was not made to capitalize

*Gunfight at the O.K. Corral.* **Burt Lancaster and players.**

on it; and approached the material in an entirely different way."

In effect, the new production, which had temporary working titles of *The Law and Tombstone,* then *Day of the Guns,* attempted to tell the *true* story of the O.K. Corral and what happened *afterward*. Naturally, Sturges, who also produced, allowed some dramatic license, but, for the most part, the events depicted were factual.

Edward Anhalt's screenplay for the United Artists release was based on *Tombstone's Epitaph,* a book by Douglas D. Martin, which utilized actual bulletins from that town's newspaper. The film opened with the *accurately* staged gunfight (the *conclusion* of all other Earp/Holliday movies), and was followed by the trial of the Earps for the murders of the McLowerys and Billy Clanton. Sturges explains the remainder of the story, which was set during the six months succeeding the lawmen's acquittal: "Ike Clanton sought revenge for the O.K. Corral by having his men ambush Earp's two brothers, killing one and maiming the other. Unwittingly, by sponsoring these deeds, the outlaw had turned the first spadeful of earth on his own grave. Earp's vengeance was violent.

"Forsaking a lifetime on the side of law and order, Wyatt briefly became a fugitive himself. Even Doc Holliday, ruthless as any man in frontier history, was shaken by the running amok of Earp, a man he'd thought of as a demigod.

"After Earp had coldly wiped out those responsible for his brothers' fate, he took no hypocrite's alibi; instead he took off his guns and his badge and never wore them again."

*Hour of the Gun* was basically a "chase" picture, depicting how Earp (James Garner), with the help of Holliday (Jason Robards), and a posse, tracked down and killed the four assassins and, finally, the man who'd hired them, Ike Clanton (Robert Ryan). The Panavision-Deluxe Color movie concluded with the now ex-marshal bidding a final goodbye to his dying gambler friend in a Colorado sanitarium.[3]

Upon the release of his film, Sturges recognized that audience interest in westerns had diminished markedly during the ten years since *Gunfight* had

3. Holliday succumbed there of tuberculosis in 1885.

92

debuted and what "buffs" remained weren't that interested in the *real* story of the O.K. Corral. Neither were the critics too happy with the epic *or* the performances. Most liked Robards's adroit portrayal of the deadly dentist who tries to act as his friend's conscience, but, conversely, felt that Garner seemed a bit uncomfortable as the lawman turned sour. Summing up the overall production, *Variety* said: "Genuine zip and interest in first half eventually dissipates into talky, telescoped resolution, perhaps from final editing. . . .

"Unfortunately for any film-maker, probing too deeply into the characters of folk heroes reveals them to be fallible human beings—which they are, of course—but to mass audiences, who create fantasies (and have fantasies created for them) to fulfill inner needs, such exposition is unsettling."

The *New York Times* was a bit harsher: "The wonder is that John Sturges, a top director, has made such an obvious, slow film with this cast, and that Mr. Garner should be such a nobody as the legendary Mr. Earp."

This Garner/Robards starrer may have pleased viewers interested in the historical aspects of the story, but, in general, Sturges's film was an excellent example of how reality often makes for poor drama.

## FILMOGRAPHY

1957: *Gunfight at the O.K. Corral* (Par/John Sturges) Burt Lancaster.
1967: *Hour of the Gun* (UA/John Sturges) James Garner.

*Hour of the Gun.* **Karl Swenson, Sam Melville, and James Garner.**

*Hour of the Gun.* **William Windom and Jason Robards.**

*Hour of the Gun.* **Sam Melville, Frank Converse, Jason Robards, and James Garner.**

# 16    *The Curse of Frankenstein*

As Dr. Frankenstein gave life to his monster, so did Britain's Hammer Productions inject new vitality into the old-fashioned horror film when they released *The Curse of Frankenstein* in 1957.

The weird world of vampires, werewolves, and living mummys had given way in recent years to pictures more in the realm of science-fiction—*The War of the Worlds* (1953), *The Beast from 20,000 Fathoms* (1953), and *Them* (1954)—and the few cheap movies that were made in the gothic tradition offered little more than a trite screenplay, stoic performances, paltry production values, and, most disappointing, monsters with papier-mâché masks and zippers on their sides.

After the international success of their sci-fi feature, *The Creeping Unknown* (1955) starring Brian Donlevy, Hammer Productions, through producer-owner Michael Carreras, realized that the public seemed to be intrigued with movie monsters that were recognizably human. This led to the idea of bringing to the screen an all-new version of Mary Shelley's *Frankenstein*—surely the greatest "human-like" monster story of all.

Carreras's colleagues, however, cautioned him against the plan, stating it was doomed to failure. They reasoned that, although the original material was in the public domain, Universal Pictures, by way of Boris Karloff and his successors, had put their own indelible stamp on Frankenstein and his creation way back in the early thirties. Since that studio had copyrighted the makeup used for the infamous monster, nothing faintly resembling *that* conception could be employed in the Hammer production. It was, therefore, doubtful whether audiences would accept this new version of such a revered classic.

Wisely, Carreras did not try to copy the Karloff original, but had Anthony Hinds, the actual producer on the project, instruct writer Jimmy Sangster to fashion his screenplay after the Mary Shelley novel. Unlike the Universal production, which had modernized the tale, the Hammer version set its action during the mid-nineteenth century and accurately recreated the period. Another innovation was the use of color—seldom employed in horror films prior to this time.[1]

Cast in the principal roles was a company of exceptionally talented British performers, who executed their assignments with complete seriousness. Peter Cushing, an able, if virtually unknown, character actor portrayed Baron Victor Frankenstein and 6'5" Christopher Lee did the part of the Creature. Lee would later make *his* reputation as the star of Hammer's popular *Dracula* movie series.

*The Curse of Frankenstein* was directed by Terence Fisher and released in the United States by Warner Brothers. Told in flashback by Baron Frankenstein while he awaits his execution for multiple murders, the story reveals Victor as a young boy (played by Melvyn Hayes), possessing an avid thirst for scientific research and sharing with Paul Krempe (Robert Urquhart), his tutor, his determination to build a human being through chemical discoveries and graveyard thefts.

Frankenstein reaches adulthood and, to obtain a fine brain for the creature he is assembling, murders a noted scientist. Horrified at this act, Krempe tries to stop his pupil, the brain being damaged in their struggle. The Creature, as a result, possesses a deranged mind and, before he, covered with flames, is destroyed in a vat of acid, commits murders for which Victor is accused, tried, and sentenced to be executed.

1. *The Mystery of the Wax Museum* (1933), and its 3-D remake, *House of Wax* (1953), were notable exceptions.

Production values for the 1957 picture were excellent, with the WarnerColor aiding considerably in making the bloody details of Frankenstein's grisly experiments as realistic as ever. Though performances were generally good (Christopher Lee's interpretation, unfortunately, made the Creature more pitiful than monstrous), Sangster's script was on the talky side, resulting in a rather lethargic film, endowed with a minimum of thrills. The *Hollywood Reporter* said: "What Anthony Hinds, the producer, and Jimmy Sangster, the writer, have tried to do in retelling this almost straight rendition of the original Frankenstein story is to make it human. They have succeeded to the extent of making it almost unbearably pathetic and real. . . . You are left feeling not so much frightened as nauseated."

Nevertheless, *The Curse of Frankenstein* was a box-office winner and inspired Hammer to remake a number of the horror classics (*Dracula, The Mummy, Phantom of the Opera*) in color, as well as produce a sequel to their original effort.

In the eight Universal features that bore some relationship to Mary Shelley's work, the Frankenstein *monster* had been the connecting link, since Colin Clive, who'd portrayed the Baron, only appeared in the first two films in the series. However, in Hammer's *Curse*, the Creature had been *totally* destroyed and, besides that, it was not a very

unique-looking monster anyway. Thus, for this British series of *Frankenstein* movies, it was resolved that the Baron himself—in the person of Peter Cushing—would be the constant factor.

Jimmy Sangster, who wrote the first two pictures in the series, explains: "Actually, Baron Franken-

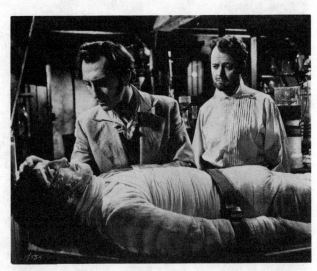

*The Curse of Frankenstein.* **Christopher Lee, Peter Cushing, and Robert Urquhart.**

*The Curse of Frankenstein.* **Peter Cushing and Christopher Lee.**

*The Revenge of Frankenstein.* **Francis Matthews and Peter Cushing.**

stein was a much more interesting character than the monster could ever be, and Hammer determined that all the stories should be developed around him.

"I always saw him as a dedicated scientist—oblivious of anybody but himself and his creation. He paid no heed to consequences, and when he did murder, it was in the name of science.

"This made the Baron a rather unique character. Indeed, at times, he could be quite heroic, while on other occasions, he appeared to be an out-and-out villain."

*The Revenge of Frankenstein* (1958) was re-

leased in the United States by Columbia Pictures. Terence Fisher directed again, and Sangster's screenplay was supplemented with additional dialogue by Hurford Janes. Color was by Technicolor.

Picking up the saga where *Curse* ended, Frankenstein is about to be guillotined for the crimes committed by his creature. But, at the last minute, the bribed executioner substitutes a priest in the condemned man's place. Later, we see that the Baron, under the pseudonym of "Dr Stein," is operating a successful medical practice in Carlsbruck, and also conducts a charity clinic, where he amputates limbs from the poor for the purpose of making another monster. One of his creations (Michael Gwynn) ultimately turns to cannibalism, devouring an innocent girl in the park. This "being" gone astray is, of course, destroyed.

The charity patients, learning of their doctor's dastardly deeds, beat him to death. However, Frankenstein's assistant (Francis Matthews) transfers his employer's brain into an assembled body

*The Revenge of Frankenstein.* **Peter Cushing, Francis Matthews, and players.**

*The Evil of Frankenstein.* **Peter Cushing.**

and, soon, a "Dr. Frank" is practicing in London's Harley Street.

*Revenge* was a far superior effort to its predecessor in every respect. Sangster's screenplay was well-plotted and direction by Fisher kept a taut rein on the action. *Variety:* "It's a high grade horror film. . . . Anthony Hinds' production for which Michael Carreras was executive producer, is a rich one. The settings, the costumes, and other physical aspects are on the level of any top production."

It was 1964 before movie audiences saw the good Baron at work again—this time in a Universal Eastman color release entitled *The Evil of Frankenstein.* Considering the genre, John Elder's script was a fairly intelligent piece of writing, although his dialogue occasionally produced laughter at the wrong moments. Freddie Francis's direction was, sadly, plodding.

This picture begins with Frankenstein (Cushing) returning to his chateau in Karlstaad, where he finds a creature (Kiwi Kingston) he created years before entombed in a glacier.[2] Aided by his assistant, Hans (Sandor Eles), he restores the being to life and, under the control of a wicked mesmerist (Peter

2. This monster, vaguely resembling Karloff in his makeup, was obviously one that Frankenstein had made when the movie cameras weren't about.

Woodthorpe), it goes on a murder rampage.

Hans follows the monster to its mountain retreat and brings it back to the castle. The creature drinks some brandy, then sets the structure afire with Frankenstein inside.

*Variety:* "Cushing plays the Baron with his usual seriousness, avoiding a disastrous tongue-in-cheek attitude, and he is the main prop in the proceedings. Some of his fellow thesps tend to ham it up to the pic's detriment."

Twentieth Century-Fox distributed the next De-Luxe color installment in Hammer's Frankenstein fable—*Frankenstein Created Woman* (1967), one of the better entries. Terence Fisher was back as director on this one, and John Elder fashioned the above-average screenplay. Supporting Cushing, who'd inexplicably escaped the blazing inferno from *Evil*, were Susan Denberg, Thorley Walters, and Robert Morris. Costumes, settings, photography, and all other technical aspects maintained the high standard of the previous productions.

After learning how to isolate the human "soul," then transfer it into another body (through an early version of nuclear energy), Frankenstein uses his technique on a pair of young star-crossed lovers: Hans (Morris) had been guillotined for a murder he did not commit, and his anguished, disfigured girl-friend, Christina (Denberg), upon viewing his execution, drowned herself. The Baron transfers Hans's soul into Christina's now-beautified body, thereby giving the dead boy/girl the opportunity to slay the real killers in a series of axe murders. Unable to stop him/her in this quest for revenge, Frankenstein finally watches his latest creation throw itself into the sea.

From a visual standpoint, Miss Denberg was certainly the Baron's most pleasing "patch-work," and her performance, as well as those from the other players were equal to, if not better than, the basic material. Discussing the film's star, *Variety* said: "Cushing could walk through the Frankenstein part blindfolded by now but still treats it as seriously as though he were playing Hamlet."

Whereas Cushing had portrayed his role rather sympathetically in *Frankenstein Created Woman*, he reverted to a total, albeit sophisticated, villain in the next episode—*Frankenstein Must Be Destroyed*, a 1970 Technicolor release from Warner Brothers. Fisher directed the complicated screenplay by assistant director Bert Batt, which was based on an original story the writer had concocted with producer Anthony Nelson Keys.

*The Evil of Frankenstein.* **Peter Cushing and players.**

The plot has Victor Frankenstein going about decapitating people, so he can use their heads in his brain transplant research. Doing similar scientific work is one Dr. Brandt (George Pravda), who has, unfortunately, gone insane before he can tell our friend, the Baron, about his revolutionary advancements in this complicated medical procedure.

Frankenstein blackmails a young doctor, Karl (Simon Ward before *Young Winston*), and his fiancée, Anna (Veronica Carlson), into helping him kidnap Brandt from the asylum. He wants to cure his brain, then learn the final steps of the technique.

Because his patient suffers a heart attack, Frankenstein decides to transplant his brain into a healthy body. This will ensure the secret's survival. The body (Freddie Jones) containing Brandt's brain escapes, killing Anna in the act, but Victor follows it to the home of Ella Brandt (Maxine Audley), the doctor's wife. There, after a brutal fight, Frankenstein and Brandt are consumed in flames, while Karl, who'd followed Victor to seek revenge for Anna's death, dies outside the house from wounds.

*Frankenstein Created Woman.* **Susan Denberg and Peter Cushing.**

*Frankenstein Created Woman.* **Peter Cushing.**

Artistically, *Frankenstein Must Be Destroyed* was no better or worse than the immediately preceding entries in this financially successful series. A highlight of the action was the rather ghastly brain operation, that had the unorthodox surgeon utilizing a saw, a ratchet, and a gimlet, and which *Variety* termed: ". . . rather more horrible than horrifying."

The *Hollywood Reporter:* "Batt's screenplay is sufficient to raise the shortest of neck hair when teamed with Fisher's effectively tight direction. There are a few moments of cliché dialogue such as the comical police inspector being solemnly informed that he has 'the crime of the century' on

his hands. But overlooking these few instances and the caricatured snuff-sniffing inspector,[3] *Frankenstein Must Be Destroyed* effectively fulfills its purpose."

In 1971, Jimmy Sangster wrote (with Jeremy Burnham), produced, and directed *The Horror of Frankenstein,* which he describes as "a total revamping of *The Curse of Frankenstein,* played for laughs." Ralph Bates starred.

Since this film did not feature Cushing and was in no way a continuation of the previous five productions, it cannot be considered to be part of the successful series of sequels.

The latest chapter in the macabre activities of the misguided scientist received a Paramount release in 1974. Flmed in Eastman color, *Frankenstein and the Monster from Hell* was, undoubtedly, the series' weakest segment. Its plot had a Dr. Helder (Shane Briant) being committed to a lunatic asylum for trying to reproduce the experiments of Frankenstein. When two warders mistreat him, he is rescued by a mute girl, known as "The Angel" (Madeline

3. Thorley Walters essayed this role.

*Frankenstein Must Be Destroyed!* **Peter Cushing disposes of "friend."**

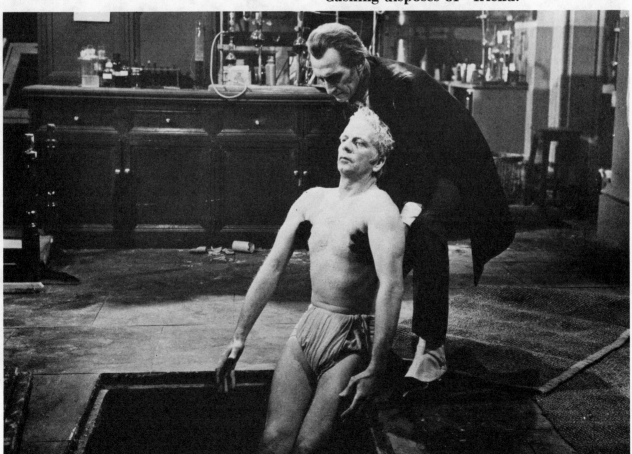

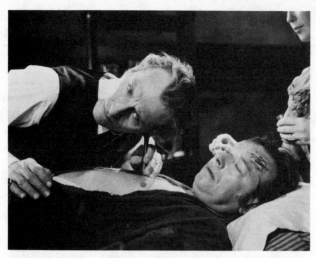

*Frankenstein Must Be Destroyed!* Peter Cushing, Freddie Jones, and Veronica Carlson.

*Frankenstein and the Monster from Hell.* Shane Briant, Peter Cushing, and Madeline Smith.

*Frankenstein and the Monster from Hell.* Shane Briant, David Prowse, Madeline Smith, and Peter Cushing.

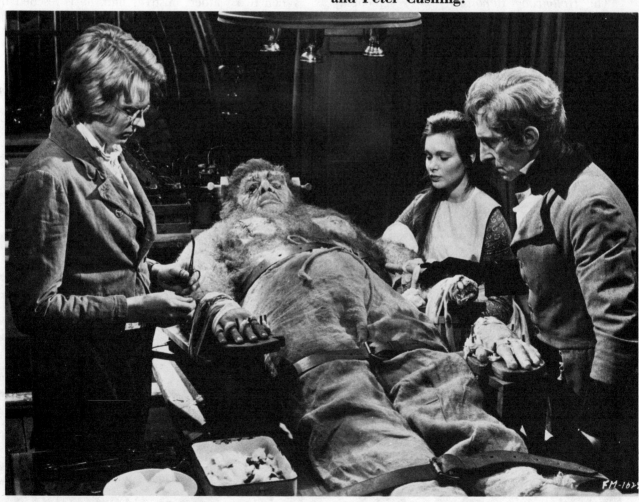

Smith) and Dr. Victor, who is our Baron running the asylum under an alias.

Victor has a hidden laboratory in which he conceals a grotesque monster (David Prowse)—made from dead patients. Because his hands had been burned in the last picture, the Baron has Helder perform a brain transplant on the creature, utilizing the cerebellum of a professor who had hanged himself.

Again, Frankenstein's plans are not brought to maturity. His monster escapes and is killed by the asylum inmates. However, he tells Helder he knows how to correct his mistakes and the pair start planning another experiment.

There was little director Terence Fisher could do to help John Elder's uninventive script, although from a technical standpoint, he did utilize the corners of soundstages efficiently enough to partially conceal the movie's meager production values—definitely inferior to the series' earlier efforts. Part of the picture's problem was its ridiculous monster, described by *Variety* as "a minature King Kong in drag." Producer on this low-budget horror excursion was Roy Skeggs.

Summarized the *Hollywood Reporter*: "*Frankenstein and the Monster from Hell* . . . is a grade-B Hammer horror film which is short on terror and long on camp value."

Although, at this writing, no further entries in Hammer's *Frankenstein* series have been announced, it's likely that we haven't seen the last of the busy Baron. Hopefully, the next time he ventures forth to do evil upon mankind, his dramatic vehicle will be as interesting as some of his experiments. That last outing was a dud!

## FILMOGRAPHY

1957: *Curse of Frankenstein, The* (WB/Terence Fisher) Peter Cushing.

1958: *Revenge of Frankenstein, The* (Col/Terence Fisher) Peter Cushing.

1964: *Evil of Frankenstein, The* (U/Freddie Francis) Peter Cushing.

1967: *Frankenstein Created Woman* (Fox/Terence Fisher) Peter Cushing.

1970: *Frankenstein Must Be Destroyed* (WB/Terence Fisher) Peter Cushing.

1974: *Frankenstein and the Monster from Hell* (Par/Terence Fisher) Peter Cushing.

# 17   *Room at the Top*

Prior to the release of *Room at the Top* in 1959, most British films that played in the United States were relegated to the "art house" circuit. Average Americans had found these pictures, in general, dull; of inferior quality to native product; and featuring actors with accents difficult to understand.

The Romulus production was instrumental in changing this attitude. Arriving in "the Colonies" amid a frenzy of claims by censorship groups that its dialogue was too raw and its bedroom scenes too adult,[1] *Room at the Top* caused a considerable furor and thereby reaped for itself a mound of sensational publicity, which, naturally, had a major impact on the box-office receipts.

But, aside from its controversial aspects, this adaptation of John Braine's low-keyed novel was a fine motion picture—with a literate screenplay by Neil Paterson, directed with great sensitivity by Jack Clayton. The performances of Laurence Harvey and Simone Signoret, who was awarded the Best Actress Oscar for her portrayal, were flawless, as were those by the rest of the cast. Critical approval was virtually unanimous. The *New York Times* observed: "*Room at the Top* may be basically cheerless and somber, but it has a strikingly effective view."

Based on the public's positive response to this superior drama, domestic exhibitors began to view English films with a more careful eye and, within a few months, the cream of this imported product—regardless of theme—was being released here on a more widespread basis.

Producer James Woolf, in a 1965 interview with Stephen Watts for the *New York Times*, recalled how his successful film came to be made: "We [meaning himself and Laurence Harvey] wanted to do *Look Back in Anger*, but John Osborne and Tony Richardson wanted to make the film themselves.[2] So we said, let's do another 'angry young man' story anyhow—and we bought *Room at the Top* instead."

Paterson's script follows the career of Joe Lampton (Harvey), an alert young man of humble background who takes a job as an accountant in the local government offices of a North Country town. He finds that this village is riddled with snobbishness and is virtually controlled by Abe Brown (Donald Wolfit), a self-made millionaire mill owner. Determined to make a success of himself (despite his low status in this British caste system), Lampton seduces the rich man's attractive, if immature, daughter, Susan (Heather Sears).

Concurrently, he becomes involved in a torrid affair with Alice Aisgill (Simone Signoret), an older French woman, unhappily married to a rather insensitive Englishman (Allan Cuthbertson). It is in this relationship that Joe finds genuine happiness and an awareness of the necessity of clinging to his own ideals.

Nevertheless, when Susan becomes pregnant, Lampton seizes the opportunity to better his social position and agrees to marry the girl. Alice, finding herself spurned, commits suicide by driving her automobile off a cliff. The picture concludes with Joe, filled with feelings of guilt, leaving on his

1. Though quite tame by today's standards, in 1959 these love-making scenes were the frankest to yet hit theater screens.

2. Richard Burton starred in this Warner Brothers release.

*Room at the Top.* **Laurence Harvey and Simone Signoret.**

*Room at the Top.* **Heather Sears, John Westbrook, and Laurence Harvey.**

film that did not rely solely on his name to ensure its financial success, his presence was considered an asset.

Hoping to again headline a hit motion picture, the British actor accepted the offer of producer James Woolf in 1965 to reprise the character of Joe Lampton in John Braine's follow-up book to his *Room at the Top,* entitled *Life at the Top.* Woolf (in the aforementioned interview with Stephen Watts): "I don't think we'd ever discussed a sequel when we made the original. I know that if anybody had suggested one, I'd have been against it. But there'll be a seven year gap by the time *Life* comes out, so at least we're safe from that scratched-together hasty sort of thing a 'sequel' usually is."

Ted Kotcheff, who directed Mordecai Richler's screenplay, also discussed the "new" Joe Lampton with Mr. Watts: "Like many of us he is unhappy with the way he lives. He is no longer on the make. He is living with the consequences of his own decisions made ten years ago and he is facing up to his own inadequacies.

"This is a completely self-sufficient story. You can come to it knowing nothing of the previous film. It has something quite different to say and it deals with its own particular sphere of experience."

Picking up the narrative ten years after the conclusion of the first film, *Life at the Top* finds Joe Lampton unhappily mated to Susan (well-played in this picture by a mature-looking Jean Simmons, rather than the too youthful Heather Sears); the father of two rather patronizing children; and miserable as the sales manager of his father-in-law's (Wolfit) woolen mill. Joe is elected to the town

honeymoon with Susan. He has reached the "top," but only at the loss of his self-respect.

Not only did *Room at the Top* win the Best Actress Academy Award, as well as the writing statuette for Neil Paterson's screenplay, but it was also nominated for Best Picture, Best Actor (Harvey), Best Supporting Actress (Hermione Baddeley), and Best Director. Harvey, only slightly known to American audiences before making this movie, overnight became in demand for Hollywood films—usually being asked to portray cultured s.o.b.s, a more-or-less younger, more complex version of the sort of role for which George Sanders was famous.

Though never achieving *box-office* stardom, Harvey worked regularly during the next several years. Producers knew he was talented and, if cast in a

*Room at the Top.* **Simone Signoret and Laurence Harvey.**

103

*Life at the Top.* Laurence Harvey and Honor Blackman.

*Life at the Top.* Michael Craig, Jean Simmons, and Laurence Harvey.

council, but defies his father-in-law by voting as his conscience demands on an important issue that will benefit only the lower classes of this Yorkshire town. Assuredly, Lampton has not forgotten his origins.

He has an affair with Norah Hauxley (Honor Blackman), an attractive television commentator,

then, after discovering that his wife has been sleeping with his best friend (Michael Craig), and that his status at work is uncertain, follows his mistress to London, where he is unable to secure a job. Ultimately, after a consoling visit from Susan, he returns home to assume the reins of leadership at the mill—but still with the feeling of being trapped in a barely tolerable situation.

Released by Columbia Pictures, the Romulus production also brought back Ambrosine Phillpotts as Joe's mother-in-law, and Allan Cuthbertson as the widower of Miss Signoret, who discloses to Lampton that his late wife was, in fact, a nymphomaniac.

*Life at the Top* was, in itself, an engrossing production, containing excellent performances from all involved. Nevertheless, the film fell short of the high acclaim garnered by its predecessor—the principal weakness being in Harvey's character, which was emasculated in the second picture. James Powers, writing in the *Hollywood Reporter* elaborates: "In *Room*, Harvey was thoroughly unprincipled, but unswerving in his ambitions. He easily bested those with less singlemindedness of purpose or those diluted by scruples. The character seems to have been weakened by exposure to success. Now Harvey is cuckolded by a weak 'gentleman,' and he is almost pushed away from the top by others. In the old days, he would have bashed them out of the way in no time. The point seems to be that success is often a sham and triumph hollow. It may be so, but it doesn't make as lively a story as that of a hyper-active heel."

*Man at the Top*, a television series utilizing the Joe Lampton character, hit the British airwaves a few years later and, in 1973, became the basis of a low-budget theatrical feature under the same title. Kenneth Haigh assumed the Harvey role in both projects, but, since the other characters and situations were completely removed from John Braine's novels, these spin-offs cannot really be considered sequels to the earlier pictures from Romulus.

## FILMOGRAPHY

1959: *Room at the Top* (Romulus/Jack Clayton) Laurence Harvey.
1965: *Life at the Top* (Romulus/Ted Kotcheff) Laurence Harvey.

*Life at the Top.* **Player, Laurence Harvey, Allan Cuthbertson, and Donald Wolfit.**

# 18    *The Carpetbaggers*

Like *Peyton Place, The Carpetbaggers* was a gusty novel, laced with sex and branded as "trash" by the nation's critics—yet made into a best-seller by the public. Inspired by the career of billionaire recluse Howard Hughes, with much of its action set against a Hollywood background, Harold Robbins's tome was said to have sold no less than five million copies.

Motion picture rights for the melodrama were acquired (for three hundred thousand dollars) by Joseph E. Levine, who then made a deal to produce the film through Paramount. John Michael Hayes, the screenwriter of Grace Metalious's novel, was set to construct a scenario (sans the carnal explicitness) from the wealth of material in the book, and Edward Dmytryk signed on to direct.

"Actually," recalls Dmytryk, "we could have made five pictures from the novel. Each character—and there were plenty—had their own separate story." Indeed, aside from the central plot dealing with Jonas Cord, Jr. (the Hughes character), Robbins sprinkled four complete ministories throughout his volume—each one dealing with the past life of a secondary character. To maintain a reasonable length (2½ hours) for the rapid-paced Technicolor movie, Hayes and Dmytryk concentrated almost exclusively on the story of Cord, Jr.—touching on the backgrounds of the other roles only in passing.

Upon the death of his harsh, drunken father (Leif Erickson) in the early twenties, Jonas Cord, Jr. (George Peppard) assumes control of the family chemical plant[1] and appoints McAllister (Lew

Ayres) as company counsel. He acquires the shares owned by the minority stockholders—Rina Marlowe (Carroll Baker), his former girlfriend, who jilted him to become the late Cord, Sr.'s wife, and Nevada Smith (Alan Ladd), a long-time fugitive from justice and the man who gave Jonas the fatherly care he never received from his real parent—then ruthlessly begins to build his financial empire, which quickly expands to include all facets of the aircraft industry. Desiring a convenient bed partner, Jonas marries whacky, loving Monica Winthrop (Elizabeth Ashley), but when she expresses her wish for a normal home life, he insists that she seek a divorce.

Cord ventures into the motion picture business at the start of the sound era in order to help his friend, Nevada—now a cowboy star. Smith has sunk his own money into a silent production and faces financial ruin. Spending most of his time with this new enterprise, the billionaire makes Rina into a major Harlow-like star and, later, buys a studio.[2] After the new sex goddess, for whom he has always carried a "torch," is killed in an automobile accident, Jonas builds a new screen personality in Jennie Denton (Martha Hyer), an ex-hooker.

Cord's cold-blooded rise to power has, over the years, destroyed many people. Following a nasty scene in which he publicly degrades Jennie, who he'd planned to marry for the same reasons he'd wedded Monica, the loyal Nevada brutally beats

1. Howard Hughes's father had founded the Hughes Tool Company.

2. Huges entered filmmaking in 1927, producing such classics as *Hell's Angels, The Front Page,* and *Scarface.* In 1948, he assumed control of RKO Radio Pictures, selling it in 1955 to General Tire and Rubber Company.

*The Carpetbaggers.* **Carroll Baker and George Peppard.**

*The Carpetbaggers.* **Ralph Taeger, George Peppard, Elizabeth Ashley, and Arthur Franz.**

some sense into him, then makes Jonas realize that the reason he's been such an emotionally unstable "heel" is because he believes that genes of insanity are within him—as they were with his twin brother, who'd died at age nine. Smith convinces Cord that his fears are groundless and the picture ends with the tycoon seeking a reconciliation with Monica and their young daughter.

The movie version of *The Carpetbaggers* contained several new elements that weren't in the original book. Dmytryk elaborates: "We felt that Jonas Cord, Jr., needed a motivation for being an s.o.b. that the average person would understand and that's why we added the subplot about his insane brother. It was his 'chink in the armor' and explained somewhat his cruel acts.

"The climactic fight between Nevada and Jonas was inserted because Robbins's book lacked a strong final confrontation—which was necessary for our picture. Frankly, I wanted to end the movie there—with the bloodied and beaten Jonas looking at himself in the broken mirror, but Joe Levine wanted

*The Carpetbaggers.* **Martha Hyer and George Peppard.**

*The Carpetbaggers.* **Alan Ladd and George Peppard.**

a happy ending, so we added the last scene with Cord getting back together with his wife. I argued against this choice, because I felt that what Nevada had said wasn't enough to change Jonas. He might have thought about it for five minutes, but then he'd just have gone back to his old mean self."

Competently directed and performed, with lush production values, the episodic motion picture, nevertheless, received mixed reviews. The *Hollywood Reporter:* "The picture itself, directed with sharp skill by Edward Dmytryk, is exceptionally well cast. . . . What, in the book, became preposterous and incredible, Hayes has deleted. He has contributed some sharp and astringent humor, and a neat and tidy construction. The story is essentially the same, but it has been vastly improved over the original."

More typical, however, were comments such as those in the *New York Times* regarding the film's hero: "He is a thoroughly mechanical movie puppet, controlled by a script-writer's strings. . . . each successive episode in the character's crude and cruel

108

*Nevada Smith.* **Brian Keith and Ste McQueen.**

career is manufactured claptrap, superficial and two-dimensional."

Despite the critical remarks, *The Carpetbaggers* became the fourth highest grossing picture of 1964 (after *Mary Poppins, My Fair Lady,* and *Goldfinger*), with total domestic returns of $15.5 million.

Even before the screenplay for the parent picture was completed, Joe Levine had laid plans to produce a sequel—based on the most filmable minisection of Robbins's original book—*Nevada Smith*. That story told of how young Max Sand (alias Nevada Smith), the future "spiritual" father of Jonas Cord, Jr., sought revenge for the torture slayings of his parents by a trio of desperados. Pursuing the murderers for many years, Nevada kills the first man during a knife fight in a corral, then sometime later, learns the second is serving on a chain gang. He gets himself incarcerated along with his prey and, during an escape, does him in also. The final fugitive is located in California, but having matured and sickened of killing, Smith satisfies his sense of justice by crippling the man, then joining traveling gunsmith Jonas Cord, Sr., who, early in his travels, had tutored the youth in the use of weapons.

All of the elements necessary to ensure both a critical and financial success were assembled by executive producer Levine for this 1966 Paramount release. John Michael Hayes was, again, set to script and veteran Henry Hathaway was signed as producer/director.

Casting was also exceptional. Steve McQueen starred in the title role,[3] supported by Karl Malden, Arthur Kennedy, and Martin Landau as the three men who had slaughtered his family. Brian Keith (a good physical match for Leif Erickson) essayed the fatherly Cord, Sr., and one can only surmise that, from the standpoint of character development, it was the later tragedy concerning Jonas, Jr.'s, brother that caused him to deteriorate into the rather distasteful person in *The Carpetbaggers*. The film's brief romantic interludes were supplied by Suzanne Pleshette, as a Cajun girl, and Janet Margolin, playing an Indian prostitute.

But, something went wrong with the potentially exciting chase story. In spite of the talented personnel involved and an abundance of Technicolor scenery, *Nevada Smith* was a disappointment. True, performances were, generally, colorful and some of the action sequences were quite effective, yet a rambling screenplay by Hayes and Hathaway's surprisingly languid direction ultimately made this film a bore.

3. Ladd, who would have been too old for the part anyway, died prior to the release of *The Carpetbaggers*.

It was a shame, since with more care in these vital creative areas, or, possibly, even some tighter editing, this handsome western—with its universal themes of revenge and the maturing of youth—could have become a minor classic of the genre, instead of just a box-office winner ($5.5 million domestic gross).

The *New York Times:* "Mr. Hayes, the screen-writer, and Mr. Levine, the executive producer, may actually have short-changed themselves. From the way *Nevada Smith* goes on and on, it seems they might have got at least two more films—and maybe three—out of the flashback source material. To para-phrase the ads: 'Now a name . . . soon a legend . . . and eventually a television series.' "

A series pilot based on *Nevada Smith* was, in fact, produced in 1975, but it did not sell.

The final three minisagas in *The Carpetbaggers* (Rina Marlowe, Jennie Denton, and David Woolf)[4]

4. Played by Tom Lowell, this role was reduced to little more than a bit in the 1964 picture.

have never been filmed and, at this writing, there are no plans to do so. Obviously, Mr. Levine believes in quitting while he's ahead—at the box-office.

## FILMOGRAPHY

1964: *Carpetbaggers, The* (Par/Edward Dmy-tryk) George Peppard.
1966: *Nevada Smith* (Par/Henry Hathaway) Steve McQueen.

*Nevada Smith.* **Steve McQueen and Arthur Kennedy.**

*Nevada Smith.* **Pat Hingle and Steve McQueen.**

# 19  *Harper*

Lew Archer, novelist Ross MacDonald's popular private detective hero, had entertained mystery buffs for years before he finally reached the motion picture screen in 1966—and, even then, his appearance was made under a pseudonym.

This had been MacDonald's choice. When producers Jerry Gershwin and Elliott Kastner purchased the rights to the author's *The Moving Target* for a Warner Brothers release, part of the deal specified that, in the film, the name of the detective must be changed, since MacDonald was reserving the Archer handle for a possible future television series.[1] Hence, for the movies, sardonic Lew Archer—as played by star Paul Newman—became cynical loser Lew Harper, scratching out a living as a Los Angeles-based private eye.

Shot in Technicolor and Panavision, *Harper* was endowed with a tightly written screenplay by William Goldman, fast-paced direction from Jack Smight, and some memorable performances by a talented all-star cast. Many critics made comparisons between the picturesque production and Howard Hawks's 1946 classic, *The Big Sleep*, calling Newman a "modern-day Bogart."

The complicated caper opens with gumshoe Harper driving to a small, exclusive California town to be hired by paralyzed rich bitch Mrs. Sampson (icily played by Lauren Bacall, co-star with her late husband, Bogie, of the aforementioned Hawks picture), whose multimillionaire husband is missing. The sleuth had been recommended for the job by his old friend, the family's shy attorney, Albert Graves (Arthur Hill).

In unraveling the disappearance, which we soon learn is, in fact, a kidnapping, Harper gets shot at, beaten (more than once) by thugs, and meets a series of bizarre and amusing characters: Claude (Strother Martin), the religious nut whose mountain retreat fronts for a wetback smuggling operation, operated by Dwight Troy (Robert Webber), husband of fat, drunken, ex-movie starlet, Fay Estabrook (Shelley Winters); Alan Traggert (Robert Wagner), the Sampson's private pilot, who is the boyfriend of junkie piano bar entertainer Betty Fraley (Julie Harris); and Miranda Sampson (Pamela Tiffin), the victim's spoiled daughter. Harper also—unsuccessfully—tries to effect a reconciliation with his estranged wife (Janet Leigh) during the picture's two-hour running time.

Keeping several jumps ahead of the less-than-brilliant sheriff (Harold Gould), the sleuth determines that the kidnapping was executed by Miss Fraley and Traggert. He forces the woman (her boyfriend had been killed by Graves, who'd observed him holding a gun on Harper) to take him to where Sampson is hidden—an abandoned freighter—but, after being knocked out, awakens to find the wealthy man slain.

Betty Fraley is killed in a high-speed auto chase; Harper recovers the paid ransom money from a frozen food locker; and the true murderer of Sampson is revealed at movie's end in a surprise twist. As to the guilty party's fate, this is, happily, left unresolved.

Critical reaction to the production was mixed. The *New York Times* said: "The action is swift and the mystery fetching in this handsomely made color film. But eventually it seems a bit too obvious, imitative, old-fashioned and, worst of all, stale."

1. A poorly conceived and executed televersion of "Archer" starring Brian Keith debuted in January of 1975, but was cancelled after the first few episodes.

Nevertheless, Newman's personal reviews were good and, of greater significance, the production did extremely well at the box-office (nearly $6 million domestic). It was by far the most successful film the actor had appeared in for some time and provided a needed boost for his slightly sagging career.

*Harper*. **Janet Leigh and Paul Newman.**

*Harper*. **Paul Newman and Shelley Winters.**

Intrigued with *Harper*'s good fortune, Filmways Productions obtained the rights to *The Chill*, another Lew Archer novel, as well as the "right of first refusal" to purchase the other books in MacDonald's series. Subject to approving the screenplay, both director Smight and Newman agreed to repeat their previous assignments for this sequel to the Warners hit. The actor with the baby blue eyes frankly admitted that the character of the fictional detective was one that he enjoyed playing because he could have fun with it.

Unfortunately, a workable script was never achieved and Filmways eventually dropped the project.

A few years passed before producers Lawrence Turman and David Foster bought another Archer mystery, *The Drowning Pool* (after Filmways declined to exercise its option), and set Newman to again play the detective—renamed Dave Ryan this time. (Working title for the film was *Ryan's the Name*.) Explains Foster: "When we first purchased the book, Larry and I weren't sure as to whether we should call our hero 'Harper' and thereby become a 'sequel' to the earlier film. Sequels rarely fare well, so we decided to go with a brand new name, while still retaining the Archer/Harper characterization.

"A few weeks into preproduction, we realized that it was foolish to make this change, since both reviewers and audiences would recognize the private eye as Harper anyway. Warners had taken a poll of moviegoers which determined that there was a strong memory retention with the public of Newman as Harper. Thus, by utilizing that name, we had a better box-office prospect than by going with the untried name of 'Ryan.'"

Set to co-star with Newman in *The Drowning Pool* (1975) was his wife, Joanne Woodward, Tony Franciosa, and Murray Hamilton. Stuart Rosenberg directed the Technicolor Warner Brothers release, which had a screenplay by Tracy Keenan Wynn, Lorenzo Semple, Jr., and Walter Hill.

"We only made one significant change from MacDonald's novel," recalls Foster, "and that switch —one of locale—was suggested by Mrs. Newman.

"In one of our early meetings, Joanne said: 'Why do all private-eye movies have to take place in California?' We thought about this and realized that she was right—*The Maltese Falcon, Murder, My Sweet, The Big Sleep,* and all of Ross MacDonald's stories are set in California.

"Then, Joanne, who was raised in the South, mentioned that all of the physical elements needed for this film—oil wells, stately mansions, and so forth—could be found in Louisiana . . . around the New Orleans area. And, that's where we wound up making the picture."

This plot has Harper being summoned to a small community outside of New Orleans by Iris Devereaux (Woodward), an old flame, who is being blackmailed by an extortionist who threatens to tell the woman's homosexual husband (Richard Deer) and wealthy despotic mother-in-law, Olivia (Coral Browne), about her extramarital love affairs. Again, MacDonald has provided an odd cast of characters: Broussard (Franciosa), the police official with an overly protective interest toward the Devereauxes; Franks (Richard Jaeckel), a crooked cop, who moonlights as a hit man; Kilbourne (Hamilton), the evil millionaire out to get the Devereauxes' rich oil lands; Mavis (Gail Strickland), his less-than-faithful wife; Gretchen (Linda Haynes), a helpful hooker; Pat Reavis (Andy Robinson), the Devereauxes' ex-chauffeur and chief suspect in the blackmail plot; and last, but *definitely* not least, Schuyler (Melaine Griffith), Iris's devious teenage daughter.

When Olivia is found murdered, all clues point to Reavis, but, after being apprehended by Harper, the young man is shot down by three masked killers. From that point, the story becomes increasingly more complex, resulting in an offbeat climax where-

*Harper.* **Paul Newman and Robert Wagner.**

*The Drowning Pool.* **Joanne Woodward and Paul Newman.**

by the detective and Mavis are imprisoned in an abandoned mental asylum hydrotherapy room by arch-villain Kilbourne, who wants to force Harper into disclosing the location of a "black book" that details political payoffs. Left alone, the two captives attempt to escape their prison by flooding the room, then treading water until they can get out through a skylite—a plan that nearly backfires.

Kilbourne, the architect of Reavis's slaying, is shot down by his wife—in "self-defense." However, *he* had nothing to do with Olivia Devereaux's death and the revelation of her murderer's identity, who was also responsible for the blackmail threat, makes an ironic conclusion for this above-average mystery.

Critics were less than kind to the Warners release, which was compared unfavorably to *Harper. Variety* said: "*The Drowning Pool* proves you can't go home again. . . . This film is stylish, improbable, entertaining, superficial, well cast, and totally synthetic. . . .

113

"Stuart Rosenberg's direction is functional and unexciting."

Writing in the *Hollywood Reporter*, Arthur Knight commented: ". . . *The Drowning Pool* is one of those studio-prized packages that would seem to have every element for a sure-fire success firmly in place—every element, that is, except flair, imagination and daring."

Perhaps these reviewers were a bit too harsh with the Turman/Foster production. True, matched against *Harper*, the picture must take a second position because of a sometimes clumsy screenplay and its pedestrian direction. On the other hand, audiences who did see it still found the mystery to be diverting, enjoyable movie fare and it was a pleasure to watch Newman reprise as the likable sleuth.

Certainly, a third appearance by the actor in this role would be welcomed by his fans, as well as mystery buffs in general.

## FILMOGRAPHY

1966: *Harper* (WB/Jack Smight) Paul Newman.
1975: *Drowning Pool, The* (WB/Stuart Rosenberg) Paul Newman.

**The Drowning Pool. Paul Newman and Tony Franciosa.**

**The Drowning Pool. Paul Newman and Murray Hamilton.**

114

# 20  *Hawaii*

The preproduction problems that faced *Hawaii* were not too dissimilar from those that plagued *The Robe*. Like the first CinemaScope feature, this 1966 release was based on a prestige book, purchased for the movies prior to its publication, but delayed in its actual filming for a number of years.

The Mirisch Corporation acquired James A. Michener's epic novel, which spanned more than twenty centuries, in 1959—for the then-record sum of six hundred thousand dollars. With Fred Zinnemann committed as director, the plan was to transfer the work to the screen in two separate movies—shot back to back—with production to begin in 1960. Total budget for the duo was in the neighborhood of twenty million, with financing and distribution to come from United Artists.

But, the fictionalized history of our fiftieth state was not to be filmed as originally conceived. Indeed, it almost didn't get made at all.

At first, there were script problems. One abandoned version of *Hawaii* supposedly cost about two hundred thousand dollars, after which Dalton Trumbo was brought in—for a six digit salary—to start anew.

In the meantime, United Artists was having second thoughts about committing such a large dollar figure to this project, since two of their other big budget productions—*It's a Mad, Mad, Mad, Mad World* and *The Greatest Story Ever Told*—were costing far more than had been anticipated. Ergo, rather than dropping the venture altogether, maybe it would be better to have only one movie adapted from Michener's book—budgeted in the $10 million range.

This decision made, Mr. Zinnemann and the brothers Mirisch were forced to decide what portions of the massive novel would be covered in the film, which would have an approximate running time of three hours. The initial thinking was to eliminate the material in the first picture (dealing with the arrival on the islands of the New England missionaries) completely, and concentrate on the Chinese/Japanese migrations. Nevertheless, this design was also to change.

April of 1964—five years after the novel's purchase—found director Zinnemann exiting the project, due to "differences in opinion," and George Roy Hill set to replace him. It was still another year, however, before cameras actually started to roll on *Hawaii*.

When principal photography did commence on this DeLuxe Color/Panavision historical drama, the final screenplay by Trumbo and Daniel Taradash dealt, primarily, with the New England missionaries, but also had some sequences involving the Chinese. The Mirisch brothers had reasoned that it was better to go ahead with the *first* part of their abandoned two-picture venture, because if that film was a success, they could always do the remainder of the tome later.

Signed to star were Julie Andrews, Max Von Sydow (Audrey Hepburn and Alec Guinness had previously been penciled-in for these roles), and Richard Harris, with the likes of Gene Hackman and Carroll O'Connor playing supporting assignments. A one-hundred-twenty-day schedule was set, with shooting to take place off Norway, in New England, Hollywood, Tahiti, and, finally, Hawaii.

Production did not proceed without numerous problems, and it wasn't long before the picture was far behind schedule. In August of 1965, with two-thirds of the budgeted shooting time elapsed, only one-third of the movie was in the can. Fearing that

*Hawaii*. The missionaries arrive.

*Hawaii*. Max von Sydow and Julie Andrews.

the originally set negative cost of $10 million might climb to fourteen, Arthur Hiller was tentatively set to assume the directorial reins, and, in this regard, company executive Marvin Mirisch flew to Hawaii for conferences with his producer brother, Walter, and George Roy Hill. A day later, the trade was

informed that Mr. Hill would remain on the picture, but to help compensate for the enlarged expenses, part of the screenplay (that dealing with the Chinese) would be cut.

Final negative cost on the movie was approximately $15 million.

The United Artists release was, essentially, a story of the nonviolent destruction of one culture by another. Following a brief, but effective, prologue, detailing the origin of the Hawaiian peoples, the film moves to New England of 1820, where we meet Abner Hale (Von Sydow), a young and overzealous Protestant missionary, and Jerusha Bromley (Miss Andrews), the charming young girl from a good family, who weds the Reverend when she believes her sea captain beau, Rafer Hoxworth (Harris), has forgotten her.

The Hales, along with a number of other missionary families, are sent to the Hawaiian islands to bring "God's word" to the simple, friendly inhabitants. Shocked by what he finds—bare-breasted maidens, widespread incest, and pagan idols—Abner begins his often cruel campaign to convert these people to our Puritan heritage. Ruler of the community is Malama (Jocelyne LaGarde), and it is because of

116

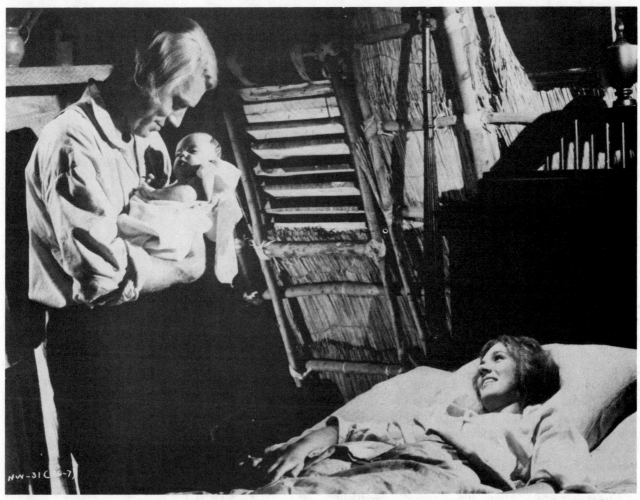

*Hawaii.* **Max von Sydow and Julie Andrews.**

*Hawaii.* **Richard Harris, Ted Nobriga, and Jocelyne LaGarde.**

her friendship for the warm Jerusha that she gradually discards her centuries-old customs for those of the West—even to the point of "divorcing" her brother/husband, Kelolo (Ted Nobriga). If this were not enough, the missionaries also bring disease to Hawaii and, thereby, kill hundreds of the non-immune natives.

In the Hale's personal lives, trouble erupts when Hoxworth and his boisterous crew arrive on the islands. Rafer is surprised to learn that his true love—now pregnant—is married to this weakling minister and, throughout the remainder of the picture, remains Abner's severest critic. Jerusha also finds it difficult to accept her husband's harsh methods, but she continues to be the loyal wife and dutiful mother—until her untimely death from overwork and exhaustion. Though he never forsakes his religious beliefs (unlike many of the other missionaries who quit their clerical work in favor of commercial enterprise), Abner cannot help but feel tormented for his unforgiving behavior, which has destroyed the spirit and lives of so many. The film ends with the aged missionary, slightly more mellow as a widower, separated from his children, abandoned by his church, but devoted in his own way to his people.

*Hawaii* was a beautiful picture to behold—full of marvelous scenery, complemented with a rich score by Elmer Bernstein. Acting was uniformly excellent and, within the confines of the script, Hill's direction was fine. It was in the Trumbo/Taradash screenplay that the movie's principal fault lay.

As the tale's central character, Abner Hale—invariably behaving with his rigid predictability—was anything but likable. In fact, he might almost be described as the villain of the piece.

This being the case, then with whom in the film was the audience to identify? Jerusha and Hoxworth were quite sympathetic, yet neither character was developed strongly enough to reasonably expect them to prevail over Hale's bigoted ways, although, at times, one wished that Abner would "disappear," so that the two could be reunited. The natives, on the other hand, were merely pawns in the drama.

In sum, whereas the screenplay may have been rather fascinating to audiences from a historical standpoint, in that it detailed how Hawaii was commercialized and converted to Western ways, it was also a bore—misshapen in its structure to allow a minimum of viewer involvement, due, simply, to the absence of a hero.

The *New York Times:* "Not since the Rev. Davidson went after Sadie Thompson has Protestant

*The Hawaiians.* **Charlton Heston.**

*The Hawaiians.* **Mako and Tina Chen.**

Christian proselytism come off so poorly on the screen."

Released on a roadshow basis, *Hawaii* garnered $18 million in domestic film rentals, and, though these returns were disappointing in relationship to its cost, through worldwide distribution, the film ultimately went into the black.

The Mirisch Brothers knew that the second half of their Hawaii story (the immigration of the Chinese) held the basis for a strong sequel to the less-than-successful 1966 release, but it was four years before this more modestly budgeted and logistically easier film wound up in theaters.

Walter Mirisch: "We took the sequences we'd eliminated from the original picture and completely reworked them into an entirely new screenplay."

James R. Webb wrote the script for *The Hawaiians* (1970), a 133 minute DeLuxe Color/

Panavision feature, released through United Artists. Set near the end of the nineteenth century, the episodic story tells of Whip Hoxworth (Charlton Heston), grandson to the character played by Richard Harris in *Hawaii,* who is considered by his relatives—headed by brother-in-law Micah Hale (Alec McCowen), descendant of Abner—to be the black sheep of the family. Married to Purity (Geraldine Chaplin), an island lass who goes mad after the birth of their only child, the sea-loving Whip proves his worth by introducing the pineapple to Hawaii as a commercial crop.

The other central role in the film is that of Nyuk Tsin (Tina Chen), an intelligent young Chinese girl, brought to the islands for sale into a brothel, but saved by Mun Ki (Mako). He takes her as his second wife (the first waits in China for him to return), and fathers all her children. Befriended by Whip, the couple work as house servants on the Hoxworth plantation and, primarily because of Nyuk Tsin's efforts, prosper to the point where they acquire their own land.

Tragedy strikes when Mun Ki contracts leprosy and is joined in the colony on Molokai by his wife, who has left their young children with friends. After Mun Ki's death years later, the aging matriarch returns home and, with the help of her large family, becomes one of Hawaii's most wealthy citizens. Her fortune is nearly lost, however, when much of the city is burned in order to combat an outbreak of plague. Hoxworth comes to Nyuk Tsin's rescue by bankrolling her, as he'd done in the past, and the picture concludes with the mingling of the races— the proposed marriage of Noel Hoxworth (John Philip Law), Whip's son, to the daughter of Nyuk Tsin.

The *New York Times:* "The Hawaiians is the kind of film (not too rare) in which the spectacle takes place in front of the camera, but character changes and dramatic development mostly happen off screen."

Not that the Tom Gries-directed movie wasn't entertaining. As the *Hollywood Reporter* commented: "One is never impressed by director Gries' imagination; one doesn't have time to be. Gries keeps things moving. If a scene is dull—although in James R. Webb's efficient screenplay, they seldom are—one doesn't worry—something else will be happening soon enough."

*The Hawaiians* may have spanned many decades, but because of the superficial character development and an overdependence on interior settings, it was an inferior translation of the middle section of the best-

*The Hawaiians.* **Charlton Heston and Geraldine Chaplin.**

selling book, lacking the "epic" quality that had compensated for many of its predecessor's faults. Performances, with a few exceptions on both ends of the spectrum, were merely competent, with Heston contributing little more than his usual stern-jawed "heroic" characterization, so familiar to fans of his pictures. Miss Chaplin wasn't much help either, and, frankly, seemed uncomfortable in her assignment.

It was Tina Chen who garnered the acting laurels. As the Chinese peasant girl who grows into the rich, influential matron, she was superb and dominated the film. *Variety:* "Miss Chen's is a star performance, and can best be likened to Luise Rainer in *The Good Earth.*"

Mirisch: "After we finished *The Hawaiians,* we toyed with the idea of filming the balance of Michener's book—the modern story, which encompasses World War II and statehood. But, before we did anything about it, United Artists acquired our rights to the novel. I understand they're planning to do something with the book on television, but know nothing of the details."

Conceived together, but executed (with major changes) as individual projects, neither *Hawaii*, nor *The Hawaiians*, did justice to James A. Michener's widely acclaimed work. Had Fred Zinnemann's original massive, but cohesive, plan—to shoot both pictures back-to-back—been followed, might the final result have been more pleasing?

One can only speculate.

## FILMOGRAPHY

1966: *Hawaii* (UA/George Roy Hill) Max Von Sydow.
1970: *Hawaiians, The* (UA/Tom Gries) Charlton Heston.

*The Hawaiians.* **Charlton Heston and John Phillip Law.**

# 21    *Planet of the Apes*

"A movie about talking apes?!?!"

"That's a great idea . . . if you're *Walt Disney*."

Such was the typical reaction to the announcement by producer Arthur P. Jacobs and director J. Lee Thompson that they'd purchased film rights to French novelist Pierre Boulle's newest work, *Planet of the Apes*—the tale of a space traveler who lands on a strange planet, ruled by simian creatures that speak.

"Top movie producers told me I'd be laughed out of the business if I made this picture," recalled Jacobs in a 1971 interview with the *Los Angeles Herald-Examiner*.

"We had unbelievable problems getting this story off the ground," admits Thompson. "Every studio we approached—both here and in Europe—turned the project down. They felt it would be impossible to put a bunch of talking monkeys into a serious drama.

"Finally, I got involved directing some other pictures and let my option on the material drop."

Jacobs still had faith in the project, however: "I finally convinced Darryl and Richard Zanuck to allow me to make a screen test at Twentieth Century-Fox.

"Rod Serling wrote the script, Oscar-winner Leon Shamroy shot the test, and Edward G. Robinson, in ape makeup, and Charlton Heston acted in it."

The fifteen-minute piece of celluloid convinced the studio heads that the Boulle book could, indeed, make a viable motion picture and they gave Jacobs a six-million-dollar budget to prove it. One million of that sum was allotted for makeup—to be executed by John Chambers, who, for his work on this movie, received a special Academy Award. In a 1968 interview with the *Hollywood Citizen-News*, the artist

*Planet of the Apes.* **Kim Hunter, Charlton Heston, and Linda Harrison.**

described his innovative techniques: "We had to develop a believable chimpanzee, gorilla, and orangutan makeup that could be worn as long as fourteen hours at a time.

"So we experimented with a foam rubber so

121

meticulously constructed that when worn like a mask, it allows the human skin to breathe naturally under it. Then we came up with a paint—a makeup paint—with which the rubber can be covered without closing the invisible pores.

"And we also produced a new variation of adhesive which allows us to fasten these foam rubber applicances—be they full masks or just cheeks, chins, brows, lips, or even ears—to the human skin without irritating it or clogging the pores."

These advances, incidentally, had far-reaching value—especially in the therapeutic field. Even before the 1968 Fox DeLuxe color/Panavision production was released, the techniques had been used to help repair faces of war wounded.

Franklin J. Schaffner directed *Planet of the Apes* (Thompson was unavailable), which had its final screenplay co-authored by Michael Wilson and Serling. Heston repeated the role he'd performed in the test (the lost astronaut), but Mr. Robinson, extremely uncomfortable in the burdensome ape makeup, bowed out of the project and was replaced by Maurice Evans.

The basic story of *Planet* was not complicated: Taylor (Heston) and his fellow space travelers are inadvertently propelled twenty centuries ahead of Earth to a strange planet where the talking apes are the superior beings and the caveman-level humans are utilized much like we treat some animals in our society—for scientific experiments, exhibition, or game hunting.

Captured by these monkeys of high intellect, Taylor's two companions are quickly dealt with (one is stuffed for a museum, while the other is turned into a vegetable via an experimental brain operation), then he—having let it be known that, unlike other humans, he can speak and reason—is tried in front of an Inquisition, headed by the political orangutan, Dr. Zaius (Evans), who claims that the astronaut is a danger to the ape society—and must be destroyed through surgery.

Taylor and Nova (Linda Harrison), a mute cave-girl he has befriended, are helped in an escape by three chimpanzee scientists—Cornelius (Roddy McDowall), his fiancée, Zira (Kim Hunter), and young Lucius (Lou Wagner). These sympathetic

*Planet of the Apes.* **Jeff Burton, Robert Gunner, and Charlton Heston.**

*Planet of the Apes.* **Kim Hunter, James Daly, Charlton Heston, Woodrow Parfrey, James Whitmore, Maurice Evans, and Roddy McDowell.**

simians, dissatisfied with the world of superstition and oppressive thought control in which they live, have decided that Taylor cannot be harmed, and the quintet flees to the Forbidden Zone—a place where no ape may venture.

Zaius and his henchmen pursue the group, but Taylor captures his adversary, who indicates that *he* has been to the Forbidden Zone and is aware of the terrible secret it holds. The chimps—promised by Zaius that they will not be dealt with *too* harshly—decide to remain with their own kind, so Taylor and Nova journey alone into the mysterious no-man's-land.

The conclusion of the film is a true shocker—with the humans coming upon the head of what was once the Statue of Liberty. Obviously, Taylor is on Earth —two thousand years hence. Man has destroyed himself through nuclear war and, subsequently, has become a being inferior to the apes.

Audiences and critics had one of two basic re-

actions to Jacobs' science-fiction entertainment: love or hate. The *New York Times:* "It is no good at all, but fun, at moments, to watch."

Happily for the producer, who'd really staked his reputation on this film, sentiments were more along the lines of those expressed in *Variety:* "*Planet of the Apes* is an amazing film. A political-sociological allegory, cast in the mold of futuristic science-fiction, the Arthur P. Jacobs production for 20th-Fox is an intriguing blend of chilling satire, a sometimes ludicrous juxtaposition of human and ape mores, optimism and pessimism . . . the suspense, and suspension of belief engendered is one of the film's biggest assets."

With its exteriors filmed in Utah and Arizona, *Planet* was a handsome production, featuring strong performances by both Heston and his talented supporting cast of "monkeys." Outstanding also was Schaffner's direction and the exciting, if disturbing, screenplay by Wilson and Serling. But, the real star of the picture was makeup artist John Chambers, whose contribution—more than any other single factor—was responsible for the motion picture's garnering a domestic gross of fifteen million dollars.

The less-than-totally resolved conclusion of *Planet of the Apes*, coupled with its financial returns, convinced Richard Zanuck that Mr. Jacobs should plan a sequel, and a budget of $4.5 million was allotted for this purpose. (Jacobs, in the aforementioned interview: "Each sequel cost a little less than the preceding one. Once costumes, masks, and sets were established, we didn't have those tremendous expenses. On the first film, we had 150 makeup men working at one time. The cost was unbelievable.")

A logical plot premise for the follow-up was to develop Taylor and Nova's adventures in the Forbidden Zone, but, unfortunately, Charlton Heston was not interested in *headlining* such a project. As a favor to Jacobs, however, he did agree to reprise his original role *briefly* (one week of filming), so that the scripters could bring the character to a logical resolution. So, a new spaceman—Brent (James Franciscus)—was introduced into the action to fill the void left by Heston in the balance of the picture.

Paul Dehn wrote the screenplay for *Beneath the Planet of the Apes* (working titles were *Planet of the Apes Revisited* and *Planet of the Men*) from a story he'd developed with Mort Abrahams. Direction of the 1970 DeLuxe color/Panavision release was by Ted Post. Aside from Heston, other characters from the initial film who repeated were Kim Hunter, Linda Harrison, and Maurice Evans. Actor David Watson portrayed the part of Cornelius because Roddy McDowall was working on another picture.

Beginning with the final few minutes of *Planet*, the new film then follows Taylor and Nova as they roam the vast wasteland, climaxing the sequence with the astronaut's sudden disappearance.

Brent, another space explorer from our time, who, in searching for the missing Taylor, has also crash-landed, meets up with Nova. She, in turn, introduces him to Zira and Cornelius—now married—and they direct Brent to the Forbidden Zone, where he goes with the cavegirl in quest of his predecessor.

Meanwhile, Ursus (James Gregory), a military-oriented gorilla, leads a holy war on the unknown inhabitants of the Forbidden Zone. Dr. Zaius also goes along on the journey.

These people, who dwell in the remnants of New York City, cover their faces with masks depicting their original appearance, in order to hide the gruesome scars caused by the nuclear holocaust. Possessing the psychic ability to distort the perception of their enemies, the mutants worship an atomic bomb.

Brent and Nova are captured by the underground

**Beneath the Planet of the Apes. Linda Harrison and James Franciscus.**

**Beneath the Planet of the Apes. Charlton Heston and Maurice Evans.**

group, then thrown into a cell with Taylor, who was previously taken prisoner. When the apes attack, slaughtering the "human" survivors, the trio break out of their confines—Nova being killed in the process. The astronauts seize some guns and begin fighting the simians. With Brent slain, a mortally-wounded Taylor meets his old nemesis, Zaius, face-to-face, then detonates the bomb—destroying the planet.

*Beneath the Planet of the Apes* was a rather dull effort, which never approached the quality of its predecessor. *Variety* called it: "hokey and slapdash. . . . The story and Ted Post's direction fall short of the original."

Nevertheless, it went on to a domestic gross of $8.6 million, making another sequel obligatory. As

*Escape from the Planet of the Apes.* **Roddy McDowall, Kim Hunter, and Sal Mineo.**

Jacobs recalled: "After *Beneath the Planet of the Apes,* I was certain we'd seen the last of the breed because we blew up the world once and for all."

How do you go about resurrecting the world?

Writer Paul Dehn didn't even bother with that problem in his ingenius screenplay for the $2.1 million budgeted production of *Escape from the Planet of the Apes* (working title: *Secret of the Planet of the Apes*)—the only episode in the series that truly rivaled the original in quality. Again shot in DeLuxe color/Panavision, this saga took place *in the present* and had Cornelius (McDowall returning to the part), Zira (Miss Hunter), and another chimp, Milo (Sal Mineo), arriving in the United States—much to the shock of the official military party sent to investigate the UFO that has landed off the Southern California coast. As we soon learn, Cornelius had repaired Taylor's old spaceship, reversed the directional settings, and, with his wife and fellow chimp scientist, blasted off just before the nuclear device had been detonated.

Placed under the care of animal psychiatrists Dr. Dixon (Bradford Dillman) and Dr. Branton (Natalie Trundy), Milo is murdered by a wild gorilla in an adjoining cage. Then, after amazing their human colleagues with their advanced skill in accomplishing some primitive tests for regular monkeys, the female scientist decides to let them know that she and her husband can speak, and are, indeed, their equals.

At first, the friendly ape couple, considered harmless, are treated by both the government and the public as VIPs. They are taken on a tour of Beverly Hills, attired in the latest styles, and made welcome by all they meet. But, Dr. Hasslein (Eric Braeden), a presidential advisor, fears the chimps because of their "threat to the human race."[1] When Zira announces she is pregnant, the official convinces his superiors that the fetus should be aborted and both she and her husband sterilized.

Held incommunicado at a military base, the

1. Cornelius had informed a presidential commission that, following a plague several hundred years in the future, in which all cats and dogs died, apes were taken into households as servant/pets and, eventually, rebelled against their masters and took over.

couple escape after Cornelius inadvertently kills an orderly. They hide with Armando (Ricardo Montalban), a sympathetic circus owner, and it is there that Zira's infant is born.

Eventually, the family of three are tracked down by Hasslein on a deserted freighter. The science advisor, armed with a pistol, kills Zira and the child, then is shot down by Cornelius. Dixon and Branton are unable to stop the massacre and the surviving chimp dies in a hail of army bullets.

Back at the circus, we see that Zira had actually switched her baby for another newborn ape. The picture fades out as the infant, who is being cared for by Armando, mutters: "Mama, Mama."

Critically, *Escape*, released in 1971, was quite a successful project. *Variety* called it "an excellent film . . . Arthur Jacobs' production is marked by an outstanding, award-calibre Paul Dehn script . . . excellent direction by Don Taylor; and superior performances. . . ."

J. Lee Thompson: "Although *Escape* did a respectable box office [$5.4 million domestic], we found it was the least popular segment with the public. People went to see it thinking they were going to see a lot of apes running around the place, but there were only two . . . and they were *friendly* ones.

"Therefore, to satisfy audiences—and convince Fox they should finance a fourth entry—we had to agree to write a script full of monkeys."

In *Conquest of the Planet of the Apes* (1972), Jacobs, writer Dehn, and director Thompson wanted to draw an analogy between the apes taking over the world and what might happen in a black rebellion in the United States. Picking up the narrative twenty years after the conclusion of *Escape*, we see that the country is under a totalitarian government and that apes are used as slaves—much as blacks were in the Old South.[2]

2. The film-makers ignored the fact that, in *Escape*, Cornelius had said that this man-to-ape relationship would not come about for several hundred years. (Thompson: "The budget prevented us from becoming too futuristic. In fact, to avoid building sets, all of our exteriors were shot in Century City.")

*Conquest of the Planet of the Apes.* **Don Murray, Roddy McDowall, and players.**

Caesar (McDowall again), the offspring of Zira and Cornelius, works in the circus of his adopted human father, Armando, and "Uncle Toms" his way through the prevailing social environment, lest his true identity be discovered by the villainous Governor Breck (Don Murray) and his sadistic aide, Kolp (Severn Darden), who have spent years searching for this chimp "Messiah." After Kolp's torture-grilling leads to Armando's death, Caesar, with the help of Lisa (Natalie Trundy), his simian romantic interest, and MacDonald (Hari Rhodes), a sympathetic black associate of Breck's, organizes the unjustly treated apes in a bloody revolt against the humans, ultimately taking control of the state. Capturing the governor, Caesar decides that his life will be spared, then proclaims a new era of peace . . . under the domination of apes.

Thompson: "This picture had originally ended with the apes, under Caesar's command, beating the governor to death with rifle butts, but, when we tested it in Scottsdale, Arizona, the audience hated the climax.

"Without shooting any further footage, I went back and redid the conclusion. We reversed the shot of the rifle butts coming down to make it appear as if they'd stopped—at Caesar's command—then were raised. Also, I had enough out-takes of Caesar standing in front of burning buildings so that, after they had been edited together, we brought Roddy in to simply overdub the final speech."

The lively production was budgeted at $1.7 million (domestic gross was $4.5 million) and, though rather predictable in its story line, did garner some good notices. The *New York Times* quipped: ". . . yesterday the apes conquered the planet. Now lets have a sequel called *Take It Back*."

*Escape from the Planet of the Apes.* **Bradford Dillman and Natalie Trundy.**

*Conquest of the Planet of the Apes.* **Ricardo Montalban** and **Roddy McDowall.**

*Battle for the Planet of the Apes.* **Roddy McDowall, Austin Stoker, Paul Williams, and Noah Keen.**

There was, indeed, a final sequel, but its title was *Battle for the Planet of the Apes* (1973).

Thompson: "Had we not altered the finale of *Conquest*, this picture would have begun twenty years later with the situation reversed—Caesar would have been an evil dictator and the humans would be slaves. But, the public wanted Caesar to remain the hero, so that's the way we made it."

Like its predecessor, *Battle* had Panavision, DeLuxe color, and a budget of $1.7 million. Dehn wrote the original story, but the screenplay was by John William Corrington and Joyce Hooper Corrington. Thompson repeated as director, as did cast members McDowall, Miss Trundy (Jacobs' wife), and Darden. John Huston played an ape philosopher of future generations, who set the film's flashback motif.

Essentially, the story dealt with the beginning of the ape civilization after the successful overthrow of human oppression. Led by Caesar, the simians have taken to nature—learning to read and write and trying to live peacefully with human beings. Also

explored are the first attempts of the gorillas, led by Aldo (Claude Akins), to create a military dictatorship.

The battle of the title refers to the confrontation between the surviving human mutants in the devastated city (of which Kolp is one) and the apes, who emerge victorious. The picture concludes with Caesar expressing his hopes for future peace, however, according to the first episodes of the series, this will not be the case.

Arthur Jacobs, in a 1973 *Los Angeles Herald-Examiner* interview: "This will absolutely be the last for the apes. We've come full cycle. If we were to do a sixth picture, then we'd have to start at the beginning which would be a rerun of the original."

Though its domestic gross totaled four million dollars, *Battle* was the weakest entry in the series. Said *Variety:* "Considering the unusual fate of sequels, its not so much that this finale effort is limp,

**Battle for the Planet of the Apes. Claude Akins, Roddy McDowall, Paul Williams, and Natalie Trundy.**

but that the previous four pix maintained for so long a good quality level. . . . J. Lee Thompson's perfunctory direction both reflects and sets the sluggish tone pervading the 86-minute film."

*Planet of the Apes* went on to become an unsuccessful CBS-TV series—starring McDowall—in 1974, then served as the basis for an animated children's show on Saturday morning television.

Despite its dismal demise, Arthur Jacobs' *Apes* saga remains, if nothing else, certainly the most successful film series to ever blend intelligent and thought-provoking story matter with broad entertainment values.

## FILMOGRAPHY

1968: *Planet of the Apes* (Fox/Franklin J. Schaffner) Charlton Heston.

1970: *Beneath the Planet of the Apes* (Fox/Ted Post) James Franciscus.

1971: *Escape from the Planet of the Apes* (Fox/Don Taylor) Roddy McDowall.

1972: *Conquest of the Planet of the Apes* (Fox/J. Lee Thompson) Roddy McDowall.

1973: *Battle for the Planet of the Apes* (Fox/J. Lee Thompson) Roddy McDowall.

# 22    *Funny Girl*

Ever since the death of Fanny Brice in 1951, producer Ray Stark knew that the life story of the show business legend, his mother-in-law, would make a sensational motion picture; and, with the blessings of his wife, Frances (only daughter of the Jewish comedienne and her gambler husband, Nick Arnstein), he set out to make his vision a reality.

A number of writers had already tried to capture Fanny's fascinating life in words, but with little success. *Rose of Washington Square* (1939), a pleasant Alice Faye/Tyrone Power musical from Twentieth Century-Fox, was a thinly-disguised version of the Brice/Arnstein union.

To gain exclusive control over Miss Brice's life story, Stark, who in 1957 had co-founded Seven Arts Productions with Eliot Hyman, purchased the plates from her unauthorized biography from a publisher, paid Arnstein to keep silent, then bought several previously commissioned, but unproduced, screenplays and treatments about the comedienne from various studios.

It was the mid-1960s before the producer felt he was ready to proceed on his project full throttle. Having decided to test the material on the Broadway stage before making it into a film, he set out to find a star for the dramatization Isobel Lennart had written. Initial choices were Carol Burnett and Anne Bancroft, but Stark soon became aware of an uniquely talented actress/singer, who was then appearing in the New York production of *I Can Get It For You Wholesale*. Her name was Barbra Streisand and, as they say, the rest is history.

With a singer essaying the role of Fanny Brice, Stark decided that the show—entitled *Funny Girl*—should be a musical, rather than simply a play with music, which had been the plan when Miss Bancroft was being considered. Jule Styne and Bob Merrill were commissioned to compose a score, coming up with many strong numbers, including the classic show-stopper, "People."

Essentially, Miss Lennart's plot covered Fanny's entry into show business by way of Keeney's Oriental Palace, her years as a Ziegfeld comedy star, and her marriage to handsome gambler Nick Arnstein, who, after a run of bad luck, becomes involved in a phony stock deal and is sent to prison. After his release, the couple, though still in love, realize their marriage is hopeless, and part.

*Funny Girl* opened in March of 1964 at New York's Winter Garden Theater and went on to become one of Broadway's longest-running musicals. Very quickly, Miss Streisand found herself a superstar—enchanting millions of Americans who didn't see the play, through the original cast album, her own million record sellers, and television specials.

Initially set to direct the movie version of *Funny Girl* was Sidney Lumet, yet, by the start of 1967, he had exited the project, due to "artistic differences" with Stark, who, by now had resigned his vice-presidency with Seven Arts, in order to make this film independently through Columbia Pictures. At one point, disturbed at the proposed production's cost (the final figure was nearly nine million dollars), the studio almost backed off the project also, but producer Stark was able to save this deal.

Veteran William Wyler, doing his first musical, was signed to direct the film from Miss Lennart's adaptation of her play. Styne and Merrill contributed more music, although for the revised finale, the popular Fanny Brice torch song, "My Man" by

*Funny Girl.* **Barbra Streisand and players.**

*Funny Girl.* **Anne Francis, Barbra Streisand, Walter Pidgeon, and players.**

Maurice Yvain and Channing Pollack was utilized, and Herb Ross was brought in to choreograph. The cast was, of course, headed by Miss Streisand, who, it is reported, received the highest fee ever paid a performer for their motion picture debut. Egyptian actor Omar Sharif earned the coveted male lead of Arnstein (Sydney Chaplin had played it on the stage), Kay Medford was Fanny's mother, Anne Francis was a showgirl, and Walter Pidgeon drew the part of Florenz Ziegfeld.

Shortly after cameras began to roll in July of 1967, the Israeli-Egyptian Six Day War broke out, which sparked demands from some members of the Hollywood Jewish community that Sharif be replaced. But, when Israel emerged victorious, the anti-Sharif hysteria dissipated.

Nevertheless, there were more serious problems. Reports started filtering off the Columbia lot that

*Funny Girl.* **Omar Sharif and Barbra Streisand.**

Barbra Streisand was being "difficult" and was, indeed, telling multiple Oscar winner William Wyler how to direct and cinematographer Harry Stradling where to place his camera.

In a *Hollywood Reporter* interview, Anne Francis, who unsuccessfully requested the studio to eliminate her name from the picture's credits, described the production as a "nightmare." According to the actress, her role was whittled from "three very good scenes and alot of other ones, to two minutes of voice-over in a New Jersey railroad station."

The person responsible, said Miss Francis, was none other than the picture's star: "Every day, Barbra would see the rushes, and the next day my part was cut or something else was cut. Barbra ran the whole show—Ray Stark, Willie Wyler, Herb Ross. She had the Ziegfeld Girls scenes changed—one day she told Wyler to move a girl standing next to her because she was too pretty, and the girl wound up in the background. Eventually, the Ziegfeld Girls scenes were eliminated altogether. . . .

"It was all like an experience out of *Gaslight.* There was an unreality about it."

Despite the predictions—and hopes?—of many Hollywood wags, the Technicolor/Panavision pic-

ture premiered on a roadshow basis in September of 1968, and was an immediate hit. In the *Hollywood Reporter,* John Mahoney wrote: "If *Funny Girl* appears to succeed virtually as a one-woman show, . . . it is ultimately through the effort of the distinguished film artists who have insured the success of the film by understanding that its success was dependent on the star's initial screen impact. . . .

"*Funny Girl* will be one of the screen's all-time musical blockbusters."

On the other hand, disgruntled critics took a harsher tone. The *New York Times:* ". . . the movie is an elaborate painstaking launching pad, with important talents of Hollywood, from the director, William Wyler, on down, treating Barbra rather fondly, improbably and even patronizingly, as if they were firing off a gilded broccoli. Miss Streisand's talent is very poignant and strong, but the movie almost does her in."

The public didn't really care what the critics said. They already loved Barbra Streisand and flocked to this excellent screen entertainment—filled with imaginative production numbers—to worship her.[1] For her portrayal of Fanny Brice, the actress, as expected, won the Best Actress Oscar that year—in an unexpected tie with Katharine Hepburn (for *The Lion in Winter*).

Herb Ross, who, since *Funny Girl,* had become one of the screen's most in-demand directors (*The Owl and the Pussycat, Play It Again, Sam*), recalls how the sequel to the Brice biopic came to be made: "It originated, of course, with Ray Stark. He approached Barbra and me at the same time and we both thought it was a terrible idea. But, Ray had a writer do a treatment and first draft and, although we never used that version, it showed us that there was, indeed, the basis here for a terrific screenplay."

Again Columbia took on the project, shot in Metrocolor/Panavision and, with Ross as director, Miss Streisand agreed to reprise her original role.

The script for *Funny Lady,* which was co-authored by Jay Presson Allen and Arnold Schulman, from a story by Schulman, picks up Fanny Brice in 1930, an established Ziegfeld star in a career lull, since her mentor is having problems finding backers during the Depression. She meets the brash songwriter/nitery owner Billy Rose (James Caan), who pursues her to star in his new show. She agrees with his logic ("You need a vehicle and I need a star") and signs on.

1. The star's next film—*Hello, Dolly*—cost twenty million dollars to make and bombed so badly at the box office that it almost put Twentieth Century-Fox out of business.

*Funny Lady*. **Barbra Streisand and Omar Sharif.**

*Funny Lady*. **James Caan, Barbra Streisand, and players.**

The out-of-town tryout is a laugh-filled disaster, with the novice showman's overly complicated sets, props, costumes, and production numbers making the stage literally impossible for the actors to function upon. At one point, Fanny is unable to get out of her dressing room to make her entrance because overflowing scenery has piled up in front of her door. Yet, the astute Rose listens to the more experienced voice of his star, makes changes in the show, and it successfully opens in New York.

Although she still loves Nick Arnstein, Fanny accepts Billy's marriage proposal. Their separate careers are to keep them apart, however. While in Los Angeles, the comedy star meets her ex-husband (Sharif) and quickly sees him for what he truly is—a weak, shallow man. Realizing that she loves Billy, Fanny flies to Cleveland where he is trying out a new show, only to find him in bed with his new swimming star, Eleanor Holm (Heidi O'Rourke).[2]

2. In truth, the real Fanny had called Rose from Los Angeles at a very late hour and was surprised to hear Miss Holm answer the phone.

The Roses part, with Fanny deciding to go it alone. Years later, while she is doing the "Baby Snooks" radio program, they meet again and reminisce of happier times.

Ross: "We'd planned to do the picture as a flashback from the final reunion scene, but discarded this idea in the editing room."

Several top male stars went after the Billy Rose role. Joel Grey was frequently mentioned in the trade papers as being in contention, but relates the director: "The only other person—besides Caan—who was strong in the running was Robert Di Niro.

He gave an excellent reading. Whereas Grey might have *looked* more like the real Billy, we were more interested in dramatizing the character's 'attitudes,' and, in this respect, Caan was the better choice."

How much of the story was fictionalized? "Surprisingly, not that much," reports Ross. "We took some dramatic license, of course, but—aside from 'idealizing' the characters and making them both the same age (Fanny was actually ten years older than Billy), everything was pretty much correct."

Most of the songs in *Funny Lady* (1975) were Rose originals, although John Kander and Fred Ebb did supply some additional tunes. Interestingly, the production was not really a musical, but, as Ray Stark had originally planned *Funny Girl*, a film that *utilized* music.

Sensitively directed by Ross, whose choreographic background was a strong asset for the film's richly conceived musical numbers, this well-plotted production offered two of the screen's major stars in two of their most dynamic performances. Streisand, progressing the character she'd created years before, was perfect as a woman, who, though having reached the top of her profession, finds her life to be a very lonely one.

The *Hollywood Reporter*: "*Funny Lady* is the traditional backstage musical grown up, full of charm and controlled energy. Its director, Herbert Ross, really comes into his own with the expressive gesture of the musical form. . . .

"Caan is truly a good match for Streisand. . . . Their tough repartee rivals the best of the 30's superstar clashes."

*Funny Girl* and *Funny Lady:* Two handsomely-produced, inventively-directed, and flawlessly-performed tributes to one of show business' most brilliant stars.

## FILMOGRAPHY

1968: *Funny Girl* (Col/William Wyler) Barbra Streisand.
1975: *Funny Lady* (Col/Herbert Ross) Barbra Streisand.

*Funny Lady*. **James Caan and Barbra Streisand.**

# 23   *The Three Musketeers*

As originally conceived, Alexander Salkind's tongue-in-cheek remake of Alexander Dumas's *The Three Musketeers* was to run about three hours and star the Beatles. Later, funnymen like Jerry Lewis and Peter Sellers were considered for the principal roles, but the producer finally abandoned this plan because he felt the public might resent a picture that ridiculed the swashbuckling classic *too* much.

Nevertheless, Salkind wanted his production to emphasize zany humor, thus a natural choice for director was Richard Lester, who'd previously guided the Beatles through such madcap adventures as *A Hard Day's Night* and *Help!* Lester, commenting during production: "I was approached by Alexander Salkind and asked if I was interested in doing *The Three Musketeers*, and I said 'Oh, yes!' Then he asked if I'd read it, and I said 'Of course, hasn't everyone?' He meant the original, and I realized we all had read the children's version. I got the book, all seven hundred pages of it, and by the time I had read two hundred pages, I called him and said 'I'll do it.'

"It is so marvelous, a combination of a lot of what is exciting about films. It has comedy, realism, a chance to show the seventeenth century the way it really was, which was filthy. There's political awareness, too. I'm not saying that Richelieu could be DeGaulle in drag, but it is very sophisticated."

Budgeted at five million dollars, the Technicolor epic began filming in Spain during the spring of 1973. Salkind, in settling on his cast, had hired a dozen internationally known stars—all of whom seemed to have a grand time playing their parodied roles: Michael York (D'Artagnan); Oliver Reed (Athos); Richard Chamberlain (Aramis); Frank Finlay (Porthos); Raquel Welch, displaying a sur-

prisingly fine flair for comedy (Constance); Faye Dunaway (Milady); Christopher Lee (Rochfort); Jean Pierre Cassel (Louis XIII); Geraldine Chaplin (Queen Anne); Simon Ward (Buckingham); Roy Kinnear (Planchet, D'Artagnan's servant); and Charlton Heston (Cardinal Richelieu).

Discussing the film and his very intriguing assignment from a historical standpoint, Heston remarked: "We have corrected the nineteenth century view of Richelieu in light of more modern understanding of his capacities and his contribution to France. We did not play him as a villain. He is really the most gifted man in the piece.

"The accepted view of the man comes from nineteenth-century historians who reviled him. Even the dramatists of the time, including Dumas himself, saw him as evil incarnate, so much so that in one play they would not deign to allow his appearance. The character was carried in a closed litter and was only heard to mutter 'No mercy! No mercy!'

"Recent historians see him as the architect of modern France, not only politically, but in his general attitude to the arts. He is not as famous as Napoleon, but I think it accurate to say that Richelieu made France and Napoleon came close to destroying it."

Heston continues: "Louis XIII is often dismissed as a weak and frivolous king, but I think that's unfair too. He recognized the quality of his minister and ultimately defended him against the constant court conspirators who sought the Cardinal's downfall. It was one of the most successful collaborations between a head of state and a minister in the history of politics, and it was Louis who maintained it for eighteen years."

Filming of George MacDonald Fraser's screen-

**The Three Musketeers. Oliver Reed, Michael York, Richard Chamberlain, and Frank Finlay.**

play was relatively uneventful and after the twenty weeks of principal photography (utilizing multiple cameras), Lester retired to the editing room. According to the director, it wasn't long before "we realized we would have a four-hour movie, or, to put it another way, too much of a good thing."

A decision was made. The picture would be divided in half and each part released separately—a year apart—by Twentieth Century-Fox. Unfortunately, producer Salkind neglected to inform his actors of this plan, so, when *The Three Musketeers* (*The Queen's Diamonds*) debuted in the United States early in 1974, the performers and their respective agents were more than baffled at the trailer heralding *The Four Musketeers* (*The Revenge of Milady*), which concluded the film.

Attorneys for the various stars began to negotiate with Salkind's representatives—arguing that their clients had been signed to appear in only one motion picture and if the project was to be released as two, then the artists should receive extra compensation.

The producer, on the other hand, felt that, since the second film involved no further work on the part of the actors, extra payment was unwarranted.

A settlement was reached shortly. Under the terms of the new agreement, the actors would receive a percentage share of profits earned by the follow-up, proportionate to their individual salaries on the picture.

*The Three Musketeers* was a major box-office success. Audiences loved the idea of presenting legendary hero D'Artagnan as a country bumpkin and his true love, Constance, as a bungling klutz. Lester's film—reminiscent of *Tom Jones* in its realistic production design—contained innumerable verbal and visual gags, which burlesqued the period adventure movies of decades past.

In this telling, the Musketeers are more interested in money, women, and friendship than undue fidelity to their simpleton King. Indeed, they are not above starting a fight at an inn to steal food when they run out of money. Also dealt with is the poverty of the era—with men of lesser station reduced to slavery to satisfy the monarch's extravagant whims, such as a bird hunt, played with peasants attired in feathers, who are shot down for sport.

*The Three Musketeers.* **Raquel Welch and Michael York.**

The story line of this first film begins with D'Artagnan's journey to Paris to join the Musketeers and, almost immediately thereafter, his involvement in separate altercations with Athos, Porthos, and Aramis. But, their minor differences are quickly settled and the three Musketeers accept the newcomer into their group.

D'Artagnan is enlisted by his Constance, the Queen's dressmaker, to help Anne retrieve the necklace she'd given as a gift to her British lover, Lord Buckingham. The scheming Richelieu, wanting to undo the Queen, had convinced Louis to have his lady wear the jewelry at a party, then dispatched his confederate, Milady, to England to steal two diamonds from it. Despite all obstacles, the Musketeers, led by D'Artagnan, are able to accomplish their task and return the necklace—complete with two new stones—in time for the gala reception.

The 105-minute entertainment ends with D'Artagnan officially becoming one of the King's Musketeers and walking off with his three comrades and Constance, hopefully to live happily ever after. However, temporarily foiled villains Milady, and her lover, Rochefort, are still around—waiting to perform more dastardly deeds in the sequel.

*Variety:* "A generous budget shows on the screen in fine period re-creation and inventive notations on it. Alexander Dumas' classic is not betrayed and, in fact, takes on a new depth in playing down the

*The Three Musketeers.* Simon Ward and Faye Dunaway.

*The Four Musketeers.* Raquel Welch and Frank Finlay.

*The Three Musketeers.* Charlton Heston, Geraldine Chaplin, and Jean Pierre Cassel.

usual romantic—sentimental—patriotic flourish it got in the Douglas Fairbanks version or the too regulated swordfights in the almost choreographic time out with Gene Kelly."

Conversely, some viewers felt the novelty of Lester's slapstick approach wore thin after about forty minutes and that what they'd really have preferred seeing was a more legitimate approach to the tale—more or less in the Errol Flynn tradition.

Released a year later, *The Four Musketeers* suffered from the fact that it was merely the balance of the earlier film, rather than a complete entity unto itself. Although an additional scene—involving Reed, York, Chamberlain, and Finlay—was shot for this "sequel" and Chamberlain dubbed in some narration to apprise audiences of what had come before, those who had not seen the first picture really did not have a very good grasp on the previously well-established characters or their relationships to each other. The hilarious moments were still there, such as the duel between D'Artagnan and Rochefort on an ice-covered pond, but the prevailing tone of this movie was more serious than the first.

Set against the rebellion of the Huguenots at La Rochelle, the film progresses Dumas's saga with the kidnapping of Constance by Milady, as per Richelieu's orders (the heroine is later rescued by the Musketeers); Milady's seduction of the naive D'Artagnan, then her unsuccessful assassination attempt against him when he learns she wears the brand of a harlot; and the murder of Buckingham by Milady's cohort in London. In the exciting climax at the Convent of Armentieres, a battle royal takes place between the Musketeers and Rochefort's men. Milady, disguised as a nun, strangles Constance, and a vengeful D'Artagnan slays Rochefort in the cathedral. Milady, we have learned, is the former

*The Four Musketeers.* **Faye Dunaway and Michael York.**

wife of Athos and, with the aid of his three friends, he delivers her to the headsman for execution.

All ends as happily as can be expected, with D'Artagnan escaping Richelieu's wrath when he presents the Cardinal with an embarrassing directive the latter had written, giving Milady permission to murder both Constance and the fourth Musketeer.

The *Hollywood Reporter:* "Lester's anything-for-a-laugh approach is relentlessly entertaining, but at the expense of human values. . . .

"George MacDonald Fraser's screenplay goes more for snickers than laughs, and the episodic plotting never coheres into a compelling narrative. The endless gettings in and out of trouble have an arbitrary feeling despite perfunctory exposition sequences."

Considering the critical comments on *The Four Musketeers,* Salkind and Lester may have had the right idea originally when they planned to make only a single film. Perhaps these men should have "bitten the bullet" and eliminated many of the superficial, albeit amusing, action scenes, thereby coming up with one tightly constructed production running three hours or less. The sequel may have garnered a respectable box office, but, on the negative side, it has also tarnished the luster of its predecessor by underlining the fact that they are both basically "one-joke" pictures.

FILMOGRAPHY

1974: *Three Musketeers, The* (Fox/Richard Lester) Michael York.
1975: *Four Musketeers, The* (Fox/Richard Lester) Michael York.

# 24 *The French Connection*

As with many films that have come to be regarded as classics of their genre, *The French Connection* was a project that nearly didn't get made at all. This taut, action-filled cops-and-robbers thriller, which swept the 1971 Academy Awards, was the baby of producer Philip D'Antoni, who'd purchased the original Robin Moore novel while it was still in manuscript form. Since D'Antoni's first film, *Bullitt* (1968), a blockbuster starring Steve McQueen—and featuring a sensational car chase—had just been released, he had no trouble making a quick deal with National General to both finance and distribute this new production—a fictionalized account of the largest narcotics bust ($32 million in heroin) in the history of the New York City Police Department.

D'Antoni: "William Friedkin was an old friend of mine and my first choice for director. Frankly, he was a 'hard sell' to National General since his previous films, like *The Boys in the Band*, were artistic successes, but commercial failures, which hadn't enhanced his reputation very much. After some haggling however, Billy was accepted."

D'Antoni and Friedkin weren't too happy with an initial screenplay for *The French Connection*, so they hired writer Ernest Tidyman to start anew. "He came up with an excellent script," reflects the producer, "but, by the time it was ready, there were problems with National General. They had, unfortunately, produced too many unsuccessful pictures and were in some sort of financial difficulty. An original budget of $2.5 million had been discussed for my movie, but they now told me that I'd have to bring it in for less than two million. This was

impossible if I wanted to do 'right' by my screenplay, so I took the project back on a turnaround."[1]

Finding another home for his film was not a simple task. Several other studios liked the property, but none of them wanted to spend the kind of money needed to make it. "We were in the *Easy Rider* syndrome," says D'Antoni. "With a lot of recent high-budget pictures having 'lost their shirts,' *nobody* wanted to gamble big. Studios preferred to take small risks that would, hopefully, pay off like the minimum budget bike movie had." Discouraged, D'Antoni finally let his option on the book drop and went on to do another project.

Twentieth Century-Fox, one of the studios that had shown considerable interest in *The French Connection*, became financially solvent again in 1970,[2] thanks to the success of pictures such as *Patton* and *Butch Cassidy and the Sundance Kid*. Therefore, when D'Antoni resubmitted his property, the studio brass were more than happy to meet the budget requirements.

Once the deal was set, casting became the first major item of business. The key character in the script was one Jimmy "Popeye" Doyle, an obsessive, hard-nosed narcotics detective—the fictional counterpart of legendary real-life cop Eddie Egan, who, along with his partner, Sonny Grosso, had made the

---

1. If and when D'Antoni made a deal elsewhere, he would have to repay National General for all monies they'd expended.
2. They'd previously taken a bath with losers like *Hello, Dolly* and *Star!*

*The French Connection.* Gene Hackman.

*The French Connection.* **Gene Hackman and Roy Scheider.**

actual drug haul back in 1962. Many stellar names—Brando, Newman, Coburn—were mentioned for this role, but, according to the producer, only three men received more than casual consideration: "We talked about both Jackie Gleason and columnist Jimmy Breslin—who really looked the part—very seriously before we actually got together with anybody. The *only* actor we ever did call in for a meeting was Gene Hackman. We flew him to New York and, after two get-togethers, he became the obvious choice for 'Popeye.'"

Prior to the start of principal photography, D'Antoni and Friedkin spent a total of eighty-six days working with undercover New York narcotics officers. D'Antoni: "The much-written-about scene in which Doyle and his partner roust a bunch of barroom junkies developed as a direct result of this research. Out on the streets, I saw this sort of action take place many times.

"I also wanted to have a spectacular chase sequence in this picture, but I knew that this scene would have to be both different and better than what we did in *Bullitt*. It was while we were out scouting locations that I came up with the plan to have this chase involve Doyle, in a car, chasing a killer, who had hijacked an el train."

Avoiding the old Louis de Rochemont semidocumentary treatment (*The House on 92nd Street*) for a more flashy approach, the plot of the 1971 Fox release told of New York narcs Doyle (Hackman) and Buddy Russo (Roy Scheider), who, while tailing small-time hood Sal Boca (Tony LoBianco) "just for fun," stumble onto a plan to smuggle over one hundred pounds of pure heroin into the United States. French mastermind Alain Charnier (Fernando Rey) has arranged for the drugs to be hidden in the automobile of a visiting European television personality.

Spurred on by Doyle, the cops spend many weeks watching Boca, as well as the Jewish Mafia leader (Harold Gary), who plans to pay half-a-million dollars for the goods. When Charnier—tagged "Frog One" by the police—arrives in New York, he is also tailed, but manages to elude Doyle in a subway station.

Since it appears that the case has been blown, Popeye's superior (Eddie Egan himself) reassigns him to other duty, but after an unsuccessful attempt is made on the officer's life, followed by the afore-

*The French Connection*. **Marcel Bozzuff and Fernando Rey.**

*The French Connection*. **Bill Hickman and Eddie Egan.**

*French Connection II.* **Player, Gene Hackman, and Bernard Fresson.**

mentioned car/el train chase, which ends with Doyle shooting down the fleeing French gunman (Marcel Bozzuffi), the investigation is continued.

Without the criminals learning of the find, police discover the heroin hidden in the car and, when the illicit deal is finally consummated, move in to make arrests. A gun battle ensues in which Boca is killed. Doyle, while searching for Charnier in an abandoned warehouse, inadvertently slays a quarrelsome Federal agent (Bill Hickman), then is frustrated to learn that the object of his months of investigation has eluded him.

A brief epilogue informs the audience that, with the exception of the television celebrity, small potatoes in the illegal plan, all other captured participants escaped serious legal consequences. Doyle and Russo were transferred out of narcotics to other assignments.

Although the basic story of *The French Connection* was true, most of the individual sequences sprang from the imagination of its creators and tended to glamorize the case, which actually had taken a number of years to crack. In an interview with the *Hollywood Reporter*, director Friedkin discussed the thinking that went into the development of the picture: "Everything we did was calculated to entertain. It was calculated, not accidental. Before we had a script, we laid down a format that had a violent killing in the first two minutes, followed by an attempt to kill a cop, followed by another fifteen minutes of plot, followed by a surprise and an ambiguous twist.

"We felt that the thriller had become the province of the people who were trying to make statements through it, trying to get at social ills of the country and the world. We decided to make an out-and-out thriller designed to entertain audiences according to certain proven past film successes."

Filmed in DeLuxe color, the D'Antoni production was a hit in every sense of the word—garnering not only a spectacular box office ($27.5 million-domestic), but critically acclaimed from virtually all quarters. A tight screenplay, crisp direction, incisive performances, and the weaving of New York locales and atmosphere into the story fabric itself—rather than simply having the actors play in front of these backgrounds—were responsible for the film winning Academy Awards for Best Picture, Actor (Hackman), Director (Friedkin), Screenplay (Tidyman), and Editing (Jerry Greenberg). Said Roger Greenspun in the *New York Times:* "*The French Connection* is a film of almost incredible suspense, and it includes, among a great many chilling delights, the most brilliantly executed chase sequence I have ever seen. But the conditions for the suspense (indeed, the conditions for the chase—to intercept a hijacked elevated train) carry with them the potential for failure, not of this particular action, but of all action in the great doomed city that is the film's real subject. From the moment, very early on, when Hackman first pistol-whips a black pusher, you know that the world is cursed and that everybody playing out his allotted role is cursed along with it."

D'Antoni: "Immediately after the film was released and started doing great business, Fox came to me with the idea of making a sequel. I was involved with my next picture then—*The Seven-Ups*—but, since I had a percentage of this new project, agreed to, at least, help develop a script."

Shortly thereafter, D'Antoni found he did not have the time to work on the sequel, which, storywise, had Doyle going to France in an effort to catch Charnier, and bowed out. Ultimately, *French Connection II* was assigned to producer Robert L. Rosen, who reflects on how it evolved: "Several scripts were written before we got one—by Robert and Laurie Dillon[3]—that worked. This was the treatment that introduced the idea of having Doyle become a drug addict, and, it wasn't until then that Hackman, who'd previously only expressed an *interest* in doing a sequel, gave us a formal commitment.

"Earlier versions had opened in New York, but we felt that we should get right to the main story and shoot the entire film in Marseilles."

During preproduction on this picture, an announcement came out of the NYPD that $17 million worth of heroin seized by Eddie Egan and company during the original 1962 investigation had somehow disappeared. Naturally, scripters decided that this blunder would, at least, be mentioned in the upcoming sequel, which was to be directed by John Frankenheimer.

Whereas the first picture put its emphasis on hard, driving action, *French Connection II*, also shot in DeLuxe color, was more a character study of

3. Credit on the screenplay was shared by the Dillons and Alexander Jacobs.

*French Connection II.* **Bernard Fresson and Gene Hackman.**

*French Connection II.* **Fernando Rey.**

what made "Popeye" Doyle (Hackman) tick. Journeying to the south of France to help Marseilles police find Charnier (Rey), Popeye, the original "Ugly American," does not realize that he has been set up by his superiors, who hope that the French narcotics dealer—unknown to local authorities—will spot his old New York enemy and panic.

This, indeed, happens. Doyle is kidnapped, injected with drugs—so that he will tell the smuggler what the authorities know about his operation—and, finally, given an overdose. Though left for dead, the strong-willed cop lives, but is now himself a junkie. With the aid of French detective Barthelemy (Bernard Fresson), he breaks his habit (cold-turkey), then goes gunning for Charnier.

Finding the hotel in which he was held prisoner,

Popeye burns it to the ground. Later, following an unsuccessful attempt to capture the criminals in a shipyard, Doyle and the police break into their base of operations—killing or capturing Charnier's henchmen and seizing a multimillion-dollar shipment of heroin.

As before, Charnier escapes, but, this time, Popeye is in close pursuit, chasing him through the Marseilles streets to the waterfront where, in an abrupt, shocking finale, he shoots down his long-sought prey.

For Hackman, the production was an acting tour de force. He was hilarious in the early scenes as the rough-edged American—unable to speak French and, therefore, completely out of his element in this foreign country. However, his sequences as the stripped-down human being, trying to win a personal battle against drug addiction, were brutally realistic—surpassing even his best moments in his Oscar-winning vehicle.

Despite the strong nod toward characterization, the carefully-constructed film had a goodly share of action and, like its predecessor, made excellent use of the city in which it was shot. Critical reaction was excellent. The *Los Angeles Times*: "*French Connection II* is an audience picture, bold and vigorous, opting for action rather than nuance. There is none of the lingering irony of *French Connection I*. Vivid characterizations and plot are all, and they are whiz-bang."

Complementing, yet distinctly different from the production upon which it was based, Rosen's film was an excellent example of what a good sequel should be.

*French Connection II.* **Gene Hackman.**

## FILMOGRAPHY

1971: *French Connection, The* (Fox/William Friedkin) Gene Hackman.
1975: *French Connection II* (Fox/John Frankenheimer) Gene Hackman.

# 25 *The Godfather*

Ever since Edward G. Robinson was mowed down by a hail of bullets—expiring with a bewildered, "Mother of Mercy, is this the end of Rico?"—the gangster melodrama has been popular movie fare. The true classics of the genre—made in the thirties and forties—offered audiences fast-paced melodrama, colorful, albeit stock, characters, violent action, and presented their "heroes" as slum-bred misfits, who chose the criminal life because it offered them the quickest way to fame and fortune.

Whereas Robinson, Cagney, and Bogart led a mob of one sort or another, the terms *Mafia* and *Cosa Nostra* did not really emerge on the screen until the fifties. Productions like *The Black Hand* (1950) and *Pay or Die* (1960) dealt with this vicious underworld society as it operated in New York around the turn of the century, while others—*Inside the Mafia* (1959)—were simply superficial efforts, made to cash in on the name of the mysterious organization that was always in the nation's headlines. *The Brotherhood* (1968) was an honest attempt to explore the men who made up the Cosa Nostra, but was, sadly, a box-office failure.

Then came *The Godfather*.

In 1966, Paramount paid twelve thousand dollars for an option on "Mafia," a twenty-page story treatment by Mario Puzo and, according to studio production head Robert Evans, for the next couple of years, "we kept Mario alive with five thousand here and seventy-five hundred there." The initial idea was to produce this material as a reasonably budgeted contemporary crime melodrama—without a great deal of depth. But, when Paramount's *The Brotherhood* bombed at the box office, the studio seriously considered dropping the project altogether.

Puzo, in the meantime, had completed the novelization—now called *The Godfather*—and it was being published by Putnam, with a commitment from Paramount to help in the book's promotion. Unlike the first draft screenplay, this tome was a serious study of a criminal dynasty—a subgroup living within our society, which has its own standards of behavior and rules of justice. It was Puzo's contention that the Mafia of our generation was the twentieth century equivalent of the oil, lumber, and railroad barons of America's early 1900s.

Sales on the book skyrocketed. Before the movie went into production, more than a million hardback, as well as six million soft cover, copies were in the hands of the public. This phenomenal response to the work, naturally, changed the studio's mind about its production. The previously-set two million dollar budget was escalated to six million—with instructions to author Puzo that he should now transfer the novel virtually intact to the screenplay. Helping him in this task was Francis Ford Coppola, who was also signed to direct. Albert Ruddy was set as producer. Puzo's salary on the motion picture, incidentally, ultimately climbed to one hundred thousand dollars, and he also received a percentage of the film.

Casting was the next consideration. Almost every important male star in Hollywood put in his bid to play either Vito Corleone, the sixty-five-year-old Don of one of the five ruling Mafia families in the New York/New Jersey area, or his heir, Michael. Laurence Olivier refused the former assignment, explaining he was not in the best of health, so attention was then turned to both Puzo and Coppola's prime choice for the part—Marlon Brando, who Paramount considered to be box-office poison. Yet, after the Method actor made an impromptu test—via video tape—the studio executives agreed that the role should be his.

For Michael, the youngest of the Don's sons,

146

Coppola chose a newcomer, Al Pacino, who'd previously appeared in the widely acclaimed, but little-seen, *Panic in Needle Park* (1971).

Puzo's other intriguing characters were portrayed by a team of talented, if sometimes unknown, performers, who brought a totally realistic quality to their individual roles: James Caan was Sonny Corleone, the eldest, hot-tempered offspring of the godfather; Richard Castellano played Clemenza, the Don's fat, but loyal, lieutenant, while Abe Vigoda was Tessio, the aide who turns traitor; Robert Duvall essayed Tom Hagen, the non-Sicilian adopted son of Vito and Consigliori of the family; John Cazale as Fredo and Talia Shire as Connie were Vito's other two children; Morgana King played the long-suffering wife to the Don; Diane Keaton was the New England girl who becomes Michael's second wife; Richard Conte portrayed Barzini, Don of a rival family; and John Marley was Jack Woltz, Hollywood mogul, pressured by the organization into giving a comeback film role to Johnny Fontane (Al Martino[1]), a Sinatra-like singer. Sterling Hayden

1. Vic Damone had originally been set for this role, but quit after reading part of the script. The singer considered the story to be defamatory to Italians.

as McCluskey, the crooked cop; Gianni Russo as Carlo, Connie's opportunist husband; Lenny Montana as Luca Brasi, a brute henchman to Vito; and Al Lettieri as Sollozzo, the narcotics dealer whose actions set the screenplay's primary story into motion, were other important participants in the tale.

Endowed with a splendid re-creation of time and place, the 1972 release opens shortly after the end of World War II at the lavish wedding reception of Connie Corleone and Carlo Rizzi. While the guests enjoy themselves, Vito, Don of the most powerful New York Mafia family, is discussing business matters inside his mansion. Michael, a war hero, who, up to this time, has not taken part in his family's unsavory business affairs, brings his girl, Kay Adams (Keaton) to the party.

Later, at Sonny's suggestion, Vito meets with Sollozzo. This "businessman" needs the Don's money and access to his political contacts in order to increase his narcotics trade. When Corleone refuses (he believes drugs to be evil and too dangerous to deal in), Sollozzo has Luca Brasi murdered, then

*The Godfather*. **Robert Duvall and Marlon Brando.**

*The Godfather.* Al Martino, Talia Shire, and players.

*The Godfather.* Abe Vigoda, Richard Castellano, John Cazale, Marlon Brando, Robert Duvall, and James Caan.

*The Godfather*. **Robert Duvall, Al Pacino, Richard Castellano, and Abe Vigoda.**

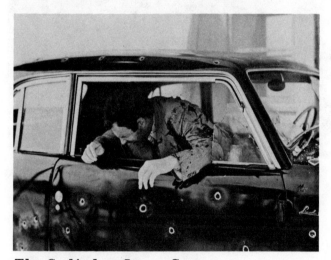

*The Godfather*. **James Caan.**

attempts the chieftain's assassination. The attack fails, but Sollozzo tries again while Vito lies badly wounded in the hospital. Michael's quick thinking, however, foils this second effort.

Assuming control of the Corleone family while his father is bedded, Sonny "hits" Sollozzo's supporter, Bruno Tattaglia (Tony Giorgio)—an act that starts an all-out war between the Mafia families. Sollozzo offers to talk peace terms, with Michael representing the Corleone faction, but during the conference, the war veteran kills both the mobster and his bodyguard, McCluskey.

To escape the repercussions of his act, Mike flees to Sicily, where he is protected by Vito's friend, Don Tommasino (Corrado Gaipa). While there, he meets and marries Appollonia (Simonetta Stefanel-

li), who is later killed by a bomb meant for her husband.

Back in the States, Sonny, upon learning that Carlo has been beating a pregnant Connie, rushes out of the family compound to bestow a thrashing upon his brother-in-law. He is caught in an ambush, however, and shot to death. Heartbroken, the recovered Vito negotiates a peace so that Michael can return home and assume control of the family's affairs. Once he is back, Mike marries Kay and they begin a family.

Vito dies suddenly of a heart attack, making Michael the new godfather. Realizing that a more prosperous future for his family lies in the plush gambling empire of Nevada (brother Fredo has been working in Las Vegas for some time), he decides to move his operation West, but first arranges for the brutal slayings of all those who have wronged the Corleones. These victims include Barzini, Tessio, who'd switched his loyalties to the Tattaglias, and Carlo, the traitor who'd set Sonny up to be slain. The mass murders make the once gentle Michael the most powerful boss in the American underworld.

*The Godfather* was filmed in Technicolor on locations in New York, Las Vegas, Hollywood, and Sicily. Producer Ruddy, in order to gain the cooperation of the Italian civil rights groups in Gotham, agreed that the terms *Mafia* and *Cosa Nostra* would be omitted from the picture, and, as a substitute, the word *family* utilized.

It was a magnificent piece of filmmaking—truly the finest gangster picture ever produced and, certainly the only one to explore with such detail the type of men who control this frightening segment of our society. Acting, direction, screenplay, and all-around production values were flawless. Indeed, until 1975, the picture held *Variety's* record for domestic film rentals—nearly $86 million.[2]

The *New York Times* tagged the three hour epic ". . . one of the most brutal and moving chronicles of American life ever designed within the limits of popular entertainment . . . the gangster melodrama come-of-age. . . ."

Not unexpectedly, *The Godfather* won Academy Awards for Best Picture, Actor (Brando), and Screenplay.

Although he'd never intended to make a sequel to *The Godfather*, Francis Ford Coppola received an offer from Paramount he couldn't refuse—one million dollars, plus a percentage for writing (with Puzo), directing, and producing the project.

2. In September of that year, *Jaws* (1975) captured the top position.

*The Godfather.* **Richard Conte, Marlon Brando, and players.**

In an interview with the *Los Angeles Times,* the artist claimed he approached the picture as "... a puzzle. I thought I had a chance to escalate the film into another area than the original, which was about dynasty. I wanted to make a definitive statement about power and to tie-in Michael Corleone's rise directly to big business and corrupt politicians.

"The finished film makes what I consider a tough statement. . . . It says that this country is in danger of losing its soul like Michael did. That power without humanity is destructive.

"I also felt a kind of vengeance in myself, a need to destroy the family. I didn't want Michael to be destroyed by another gang or by a Senate investigation of organized crime. I wanted him to destroy himself. And to juxtapose his fall with flashbacks of his father's rise a half-century earlier."

Coppola was able to reassemble most of his original cast—at higher salaries—to reprise their roles for this follow-up. Returning were Pacino, Duvall, Miss Keaton, Cazale, Miss Shire (Coppola's sister), and Miss King. Also back for a brief flashback sequence were three actors "killed" in the earlier film —James Caan, Abe Vigoda, and Gianni Russo.

*The Godfather.* **Al Pacino, Richard Castellano, and players.**

Noticeably absent from this short episode was Brando, who refused to do the scene because of a disagreement with then-Paramount president Frank Yablans.

Clemenza had been penciled-in as an important character in the sequel, but Richard Castellano, after reading the first draft screenplay, decided *not* to repeat the role, explaining: "I could in no way equate the continuation of Clemenza's character in *Godfather II* with the way he was presented in *Godfather I*. His primary trait was loyalty and, unless he went insane, or the screenplay gave him some other 'twist'—and there was none in the script I read—then he would have remained loyal throughout. In other words, Clemenza would never have made himself available to testify before the Senate committee."

The function of Clemenza was vital in the 1974 follow-up, which was budgeted at about $13 million, so, rather then drop the part altogether, Coppola changed the character's name to "Frankie Pentangeli" and cast playwright Michael V. Gazzo in the role. Frankie, formerly one of Clemenza's lieutenants, had taken over the fat man's "family" after the latter had succumbed to a heart attack.

There was another important new character in this continuation—Hyman Roth, patterned after real-life mobster Meyer Lansky, and essayed by dramatic coach Lee Strasberg, who was cast after director Elia Kazan had declined the assignment.

*The Godfather, Part II* contains two parallel stories. The first deals with the early life of Vito Corleone—from his boyhood in Sicily to the start of his rise to criminal power in New York City. Robert DeNiro, a brilliant young actor, was brought in to play the "young Brando"—speaking most of his dialogue in Sicilian. B. Kirby, Jr., John Aprea, and Francesca de Sapio essayed the early counterparts of the characters created by Richard Castellano, Abe Vigoda, and Morgana King respectively.

For the most part, these turn-of-the-century sequences were inspired by Puzo's original novel: At age twelve, Vito Andolini had been forced to flee his home in Corleone, Sicily, lest he be murdered by the local Mafia chieftain who killed his parents and brother. Arriving in the United States, the lad is dubbed "Vito Corleone" by an immigration official.

As an oppressed immigrant learning how to deal with a threatening culture on its own hard terms, Vito does well. He is forced by circumstances (he lost his job at a grocery store) to join Clemenza and Tessio in a series of hijackings, then, later, murders a member of the Black Hand, who tries to extort a "tribute" from him. Quickly gaining a reputation as a "man to respect," Vito builds his capital and goes into the olive oil business, which serves as a front for his nefarious activities. He returns to Sicily to visit his partner in this importing venture and, while there, murders the Mafia boss, who, years before, had slain his family. His old enemy destroyed, Don Corleone concentrates on widening his powerful influence in his adopted country.

*Part II* picks up the modern story in Michael's new Lake Tahoe home, where a first Holy Communion reception for his son is in progress. (Coppola: "People tell me they liked the opening wedding party in the original film better than the opening party in the sequel.

("Well, so do I. That was my point. I was trying to show how the family had lost its authenticity. I wanted to have scenes that would remind you of the first film and to show by their altered shape how much the family had changed.")

Michael is presented here as a cold, merciless crime lord, who will stop at nothing to achieve his ends. There is a considerable strain on his marriage to Kay—pregnant with their third child. Although not completely aware of all her husband's activities, she knows the nature of his business and finds it difficult to condone it. Late in the picture, she informs Michael that what he thought was a miscarriage, was, in fact, an abortion, since she'd decided she could not bear this evil man another child. The young Don is furious. Kay is exiled—forbidden to see her children.

Sister Connie, who since the death of husband Carlo has become a hardened, self-destructive jet-setter, is brought home to be a pentitent surrogate mother to her brother's kids.

Michael is also having problems with his weak older brother Fredo. Because of his own insecurities, the eldest of the Corleone siblings had inadvertently set his brother up for an assassination attempt and, when his betrayal is discovered, Michael banishes him from the family—only to "forgive" him after their mother's death.

The film progresses and Mike finds that there are increasingly few people who he can trust. Even loyal Tom Hagen, disillusioned with his long-time friend's ruthlessness, expresses a desire to move on. The modern chieftain is also having troubles keeping his sinister holdings intact. A venture with gangster Hyman Roth—who'd masterminded the aforementioned assassination attempt—to move their activities into Batista's Cuba is thwarted when Castro seizes control of that island nation. The U.S. Senate investigates Corleone's empire—with former lieutenant

*The Godfather, Part II.* Lee Strasberg and Al Pacino.

*The Godfather, Part II.* Robert DeNiro and player.

Frankie Pentangeli called in as the government's surprise Valachi-style witness, who, at the last moment, refuses to testify.

Though more intellectual and less violent than its predecessor, *The Godfather, Part II* climaxes in another blood-bath, with Michael again the architect. Slaughtered are an ailing Hyman Roth, Corleone's deadly foe since the Cuba fiasco; Frankie Pentangeli, who commits suicide in prison after Hagen promises that his family will be cared for; and, most shocking, brother Fredo, never truly absolved for his treachery.

Michael may have destroyed his enemies at the picture's conclusion, but what remains of him is a mere shell of the idealistic youth he once was. His power—for the moment—is secure, but he is a lonely man.

*Variety:* "*The Godfather, Part II*, far from being a spinoff follow-up to its 1972 progenitor, is an excellent epochal drama in its own right, providing bookends in time—the early part of the century and the last two decades—to the earlier story."

Coppola had again accurately captured the feel of the era, as he'd done in the parent production, but, this time, did it with *two* periods—a generation apart. The *Hollywood Reporter:* "The large historical re-creations work more as social comment than mere spectacle or backdrop."

Performances in the two hundred-minute Technicolor drama were superb throughout, with Pacino, DeNiro, Strasberg, Gazzo, and Miss Shire receiving Oscar nominations. Supporting actor DeNiro was the only winner in this group, although the film did capture the awards for Best Picture, Direction, and Screenplay, among others.

At this writing, it has been announced that both segments of the epic Mafia saga will be shown on television in the not-too-distant future in a new re-edited chronological form, to include scenes not previously seen by theater audiences.

Not only was *The Godfather, Part II* the most successful—both artistically and financially ($28.9 million domestic)—sequel in history, but it also enlightened many filmmakers to the fact that, done well, a continuation can, indeed, be a totally rewarding experience.

*The Godfather, Part II.* **John Cazale and Al Pacino.**

*The Godfather, Part II.* **Robert Duvall and Michael V. Gazzo.**

Philip D'Antoni, producer of *The French Connection*, admits: "Only once did I momentarily regret *not* doing the sequel to my picture, and that was when I saw how fine a work was *Godfather II.*"

## FILMOGRAPHY

1972: *Godfather, The* (Par/Francis Ford Coppola) Marlon Brando.

1974: *Godfather, The, Part II* (Par/Francis Ford Coppola) Al Pacino.

# Compendium of Film Sequels

The entries on the following pages are only a partial listing of the many films that have spawned sequels.

Every title is cross-referenced so that the detailed listing of all sequels appears under the title of the initial episode in that particular series of pictures.

Each production recorded under a master heading includes the year of release, the title, then, in parentheses, the producer or distributor of the picture, followed by the director's name. Finally, the top-billed star is identified.

In many instances, production and distribution organizations have been abbreviated. Below is a key to the less obvious abridgments:

| | |
|---|---|
| AA | Allied Artists |
| AIP | American-International |
| Col | Columbia |
| EL | Eagle Lion |
| Fox | Fox Films *or* Twentieth Century-Fox |
| MGM | Metro-Goldwyn-Mayer |
| NET | New Trends Associates |
| NG | National General |
| Par | Paramount |
| U | Universal |
| UA | United Artists |
| WB | Warner Brothers |

*Abbott and Costello Meet Frankenstein*
See *Dracula.*

*Abbott and Costello Meet the Invisible Man*
See *Invisible Man, The.*

*Abbott and Costello Meet the Mummy*
See *Mummy's Hand, The.*

*Abominable Dr. Phibes, The*
1971: (AIP/Robert Fuest) Vincent Price.
1972: *Dr. Phibes Rises Again* (AIP/Robert Fuest) Vincent Price.

*Absent-Minded Professor, The*
1961: (Disney/Robert Stevenson) Fred MacMurray.
1963: *Son of Flubber* (Disney/Robert Stevenson) Fred MacMurray.

*Affairs of Annabel, The*
1938: (RKO/Ben Stoloff) Lucille Ball.
1938: *Annabel Takes a Tour* (RKO/Lew Landers) Lucille Ball.

*Airport*
1970: (U/George Seaton) Burt Lancaster.
1974: *Airport 1975* (U/Jack Smight) Charlton Heston.
1977: *Airport 1977* (U/Jerry Jameson) Jack Lemmon.

*Airport 1975*
See *Airport.*

*Airport 1977*
See *Airport.*

*Alfie*
1966: (Par/Lewis Gilbert) Michael Caine.
1975: *Oh Alfie!* (EMI/Ken Hughes) Alan Price.

*Ambushers, The*
See *Silencers, The.*

*Annabel Takes a Tour*
See *Affairs of Annabel, The.*

*Anne of Green Gables*
1934: (RKO/George Nicholls, Jr.) Anne Shirley.
1940: *Anne of Windy Poplars* (RKO/Jack Hively) Anne Shirley.

*Anne of Windy Poplars*
See *Anne of Green Gables.*

*Beau Geste.* **William Powell, Ralph Forbes, Ronald Colman, Neil Hamilton, and Noah Beery.**

*Beau Sabreur.* **Gary Cooper.**

*Bad Men of Missouri*
1941: (WB/Ray Enright) Dennis Morgan.
1949: *Younger Brothers, The* (WB/Edwin L. Marin) Wayne Morris.

*Beau Geste*
1926: (Par/Herbert Brenon) Ronald Colman.
1928: *Beau Sabreur* (Par/John Waters) Gary Cooper.

*Beau Sabreur*
See *Beau Geste.*

*Becket*
1964: (Par/Peter Glenville) Peter O'Toole.
1968: *Lion in Winter, The* (Embassy/,Anthony Harvey) Peter O'Toole.

*Belles of St. Trinian's, The*
1954: (British Lion/Frank Launder) Alastair Sim.
1957: *Blue Murder at St. Trinian's* (British Lion/ Frank Launder) Alastair Sim.
1960: *Pure Hell of St. Trinian's, The* (British Lion/ Frank Launder) Cecil Parker.
1966: *Great St. Trinian's Train Robbery, The* (British Lion/Frank Launder, Sidney Gilliat) Frankie Howard.

**Bells of St. Mary's, The**
See *Going My Way.*

**Ben**
See *Willard.*

**Billion Dollar Brain**
See *Ipcress File, The.*

**Billy Jack**
See *Born Losers.*

**Billy Jack Goes to Washington**
See *Born Losers.*

**Black Bird, The**
See *Maltese Falcon, The.*

**Black Caesar**
1973: (AIP/Larry Cohen) Fred Williamson.
1973: *Hell Up in Harlem* (AIP/Larry Cohen) Fred Williamson.

**Blacula**
1972: (AIP/William Crain) William Marshall.
1973: *Scream Blacula Scream* (AIP/Bob Kelljan) William Marshall.

**Blob, The**
1958: (Par/Irvin S. Yeaworth, Jr.) Steve McQueen.
1972: *Son of Blob* (Harris Ent./Larry Hagman) Robert Walker, Jr.

**Blue Murder at St. Trinian's**
See *Belles of St. Trinian's, The.*

**Born Free**
1966: (Col/James Hill) Virginia McKenna.
1972: *Living Free* (Col/Jack Couffer) Susan Hampshire.

**Born Losers**
1967: (AIP/T. C. Frank) Tom Laughlin.
1972: *Billy Jack* (WB/T. C. Frank) Tom Laughlin.
1974: *Trial of Billy Jack, The* (Taylor-Laughlin/Frank Laughlin) Tom Laughlin.
1977: *Billy Jack Goes to Washington* (Billy Jack Ent./T. C. Frank) Tom Laughlin.

**Bride of Frankenstein**
See *Dracula.*

**Brides of Dracula, The**
See *Horror of Dracula.*

**Buck Privates**
1941: (U/Arthur Lubin) Abbott and Costello.
1947: *Buck Privates Come Home* (U/Charles Barton) Abbott and Costello.

**Buck Privates Come Home**
See *Buck Privates.*

**By the Light of the Silvery Moon**
See *On Moonlight Bay.*

**Captain Blood**
1935: (WB/Michael Curtiz) Errol Flynn.
1962: *Son of Captain Blood, The* (Par/Tullio Demichelli) Sean Flynn.

**Cat People**
1942: (RKO/Jacques Tourneur) Simone Simon.
1944: *Curse of the Cat People, The* (RKO/Gunther V. Fritsch, Robert Wise) Simone Simon.

**Children of the Damned**
See *Village of the Damned.*

**Chinatown**
1974: (Par/Roman Polanski) Jack Nicholson.
1977: Sequel announced.

**Class of '44**
See *Summer of '42.*

**Claudia**
1943: (Fox/Edmund Goulding) Dorothy McGuire.
1946: *Claudia and David* (Fox/Walter Lang) Dorothy McGuire.

**Claudia and David**
See *Claudia.*

**Cleopatra Jones**
1973: (WB/Jack Starrett) Tamara Dobson.
1975: *Cleopatra Jones and the Casino of Gold* (WB/Chuck Bail) Tamara Dobson.

**Cleopatra Jones and the Casino of Gold**
See *Cleopatra Jones.*

**Cockeyed World, The**
See *What Price Glory.*

**Come Back, Charleston Blue**
See *Cotton Comes to Harlem.*

**Computer Wore Tennis Shoes, The**
1970: (Disney/Robert Butler) Kurt Russell.
1972: *Now You See Him, Now You Don't* (Disney/Robert Butler) Kurt Russell.
1975: *Strongest Man in the World, The* (Disney/Vincent McEveety) Kurt Russell.

**Cotton Comes to Harlem**
1970: (UA/Ossie Davis) Godfrey Cambridge.
1972: *Come Back, Charleston Blue* (WB/Mark Warren) Godfrey Cambridge.

**Count Yorga, Vampire**
1970: (AIP/Bob Kelljan) Robert Quarry.
1971: *Return of Count Yorga* (AIP/Bob Kelljan) Robert Quarry.

**Curse of the Cat People, The**
See *Cat People, The.*

**Curse of the Fly, The**
See *Fly, The.*

**Davy Crockett and the River Pirates**
See *Davy Crockett, King of the Wild Frontier.*

**Davy Crockett, King of the Wild Frontier**
1955: (Disney/Norman Foster) Fess Parker.
1956: *Davy Crockett and the River Pirates* (Disney/Norman Foster) Fess Parker.

**Dear Brat**
See *Dear Ruth.*

*Claudia.* **Jean Howard, Dorothy McGuire, Reginald Gardiner, and Olga Baclanova.**

*Dear Ruth*
1947: (Par/William D. Russell) Joan Caulfield.
1949: *Dear Wife* (Par/Richard Haydn) Joan Caulfield.
1951: *Dear Brat* (Par/William A. Seiter) Mona Freeman.

*Dear Wife*
See *Dear Ruth.*

*Death Race 2000*
1975: (New World/Paul Bartel) David Carradine.
1976: Sequel announced.

*Diamonds are Forever*
See *Dr. No.*

*Dirty Harry*
1971: (WB/Don Siegel) Clint Eastwood.
1973: *Magnum Force* (WB/Ted Post) Clint Eastwood.
1976: *Enforcer, The* (WB/James Fargo) Clint Eastwood.

*Doctor at Large*
See *Doctor in the House.*

*Doctor at Sea*
See *Doctor in the House.*

*Claudia and David.* **Robert Young and Dorothy McGuire.**

157

*Dr. No.* Jack Lord and Sean Connery in the first James Bond film. Connery played 007 a total of six times.

*On Her Majesty's Secret Service.* Telly Savalas and George Lazenby, who took over the part from Connery for this one picture.

*The Man With the Golden Gun.* This was Roger Moore's second outing as the super spy.

*Dr. Goldfoot and the Bikini Machine*
1965: (AIP/Norman Taurog) Vincent Price.
1966: *Dr. Goldfoot and the Girl Bombs* (AIP/Mario Bava) Vincent Price.

*Dr. Goldfoot and the Girl Bombs*
See *Dr. Goldfoot and the Bikini Machine.*

*Doctor in Distress*
See *Doctor in the House.*

*Doctor in Love*
See *Doctor in the House.*

*Doctor in the House*
1954: (Republic/Ralph Thomas) Dirk Bogarde.
1956: *Doctor at Sea* (Republic/Ralph Thomas) Dirk Bogarde.
1957: *Doctor at Large* (U/Ralph Thomas) Dirk Bogarde.
1962: *Doctor in Love* (Grovenor/Ralph Thomas) Michael Craig.
1964: *Doctor in Distress* (Grovenor/Ralph Thomas) Dirk Bogarde.

*Dr. No*
1962: (UA/Terence Young) Sean Connery.
1963: *From Russia With Love* (UA/Terence Young) Sean Connery.
1964: *Goldfinger* (UA/Guy Hamilton) Sean Connery.
1965: *Thunderball* (UA/Terence Young) Sean Connery.
1967: *You Only Live Twice* (UA/Lewis Gilbert) Sean Connery.
1969: *On Her Majesty's Secret Service* (UA/Peter Hunt) George Lazenby.
1971: *Diamonds are Forever* (UA/Guy Hamilton) Sean Connery.
1973: *Live and Let Die* (UA/Guy Hamilton) Roger Moore.
1974: *Man With the Golden Gun, The* (UA/Guy Hamilton) Roger Moore.
1977: *Spy Who Loved Me, The* (UA/Lewis Gilbert) Roger Moore.

*Dr. Phibes Rises Again*
See *Abominable Dr. Phibes, The.*

*Don Q, Son of Zorro*
See *Mark of Zorro, The.*

*Dracula*
1931: (U/Tod Browning) Bela Lugosi.
1931: *Frankenstein* (U/James Whale) Boris Karloff.
1935: *Bride of Frankenstein* (U/James Whale) Boris Karloff.
1936: *Dracula's Daughter* (U/Lambert Hillyer) Otto Kruger.
1939: *Son of Frankenstein* (U/Rowland V. Lee) Basil Rathbone.
1941: *Wolf Man, The* (U/George Waggner) Lon Chaney, Jr.
1942: *Ghost of Frankenstein, The* (U/Erle C. Kenton) Sir Cedric Hardwicke.

1943: *Frankenstein Meets the Wolf Man* (U/Roy William Neill) Lon Chaney, Jr.
1943: *Son of Dracula* (U/Robert Siodmak) Lon Chaney, Jr.
1945: *House of Frankenstein* (U/Erle C. Kenton) Boris Karloff.
1945: *House of Dracula* (U/Erle C. Kenton) Lon Chaney, Jr.
1948: *Abbott and Costello Meet Frankenstein* (U/Charles Barton) Bela Lugosi.

*Dracula A.D. 1972*
See *Horror of Dracula.*

*Dracula's Daughter*
See *Dracula.*

*Dracula Has Risen From the Grave*
See *Horror of Dracula.*

*Dracula—Prince of Darkness*
See *Horror of Dracula.*

*Drum*
See *Mandingo.*

*Earthquake*
1974: (U/Mark Robson) Charlton Heston.
1977: Sequel announced.

*Edison, the Man*
See *Young Tom Edison.*

*Emigrants, The*
1972: (WB/Jan Troell) Max von Sydow.
1973: *New Land, The* (WB/Jan Troell) Max von Sydow.

*Enforcer, The*
See *Dirty Harry.*

*Ensign Pulver*
See *Mister Roberts.*

*Exorcist, The*
1973: (WB/William Friedkin) Ellen Burstyn.
1977: *Heretic, The* (WB/John Boorman) Linda Blair.

*Father of the Bride*
1950: (MGM/Vincente Minnelli) Spencer Tracy.
1951: *Father's Little Dividend* (MGM/Vincente Minnelli) Spencer Tracy.

*Father's Little Dividend*
See *Father of the Bride.*

*Final Chapter—Walking Tall*
See *Walking Tall.*

*Fistful of Dollars, A*
1966: (UA/Sergio Leone) Clint Eastwood.
1967: *For a Few Dollars More* (UA/Sergio Leone) Clint Eastwood.
1968: *Good, the Bad, and the Ugly, The* (UA/Sergio Leone) Clint Eastwood.

*Father of the Bride.* Spencer Tracy and Joan
Bennett.

*Father's Little Dividend.* Spencer Tracy,
Elizabeth Taylor, and Don Taylor.

*Fly, The*
1958: (Fox/Kurt Neumann) Vincent Price.
1959: *Return of the Fly, The* (Fox/Edward L. Bernds) Vincent Price.
1965: *Curse of the Fly, The* (Fox/Don Sharp) Brian Donlevy.
*For a Few Dollars More*
    See *Fistful of Dollars, A.*

**Four Daughters.** Gale Page and Priscilla Lane.

**Four Wives.** Lola Lane, Jeffrey Lynn, Eddie Albert, and Priscilla Lane.

*Four Daughters*
1938: (WB/Michael Curtiz) Priscilla Lane.
1939: *Four Wives* (WB/Michael Curtiz) Priscilla Lane.
1941: *Four Mothers* (WB/William Keighley) Priscilla Lane.
*Four Mothers*
    See *Four Daughters.*
*Four Wives*
    See *Four Daughters.*

**Four Mothers.** Priscilla Lane, Rosemary Lane, Claude Rains, Gale Page, and Lola Lane.

*Frankenstein*
   See *Dracula.*
*Frankenstein Meets the Wolf Man*
   See *Dracula.*
*Friends*
1971: (Par/Lewis Gilbert) Sean Bury.
1974: *Paul and Michelle* (Par/Lewis Gilbert) Sean
   Bury.
*From Russia With Love*
   See *Dr. No.*
*Funeral in Berlin*
   See *Ipcress File, The.*
*Futureworld*
   See *Westworld.*

*Gator*
   See *White Lightning.*
*Ghost of Frankenstein, The*
   See *Dracula.*
*Gidget*
1959: (Col/Paul Wendkos) Sandra Dee.
1961: *Gidget Goes Hawaiian* (Col/Paul Wendkos)
   Deborah Walley.
1963: *Gidget Goes to Rome* (Col/Paul Wendkos)
   Cindy Carol.
*Gidget Goes Hawaiian*
   See *Gidget.*
*Gidget Goes to Rome*
   See *Gidget.*
*Going My Way*
1944: (Par/Leo McCarey) Bing Crosby.
1945: *Bells of St. Mary's, The* (RKO/Leo McCarey)
   Bing Crosby.
*Goldfinger*
   See *Dr. No.*
*Gone With the Wind*
1939: (MGM/Victor Fleming) Clark Gable.
1978: Sequel announced.
*Good, the Bad, and the Ugly, The*
   See *Fistful of Dollars, A.*
*Great St. Trinian's Train Robbery, The*
   See *Belles of St. Trinian's, The.*
*Guns of Navarone, The*
1961: (Col/J. Lee Thompson) Gregory Peck.
1977: Sequel announced.
*Guns of the Magnificent Seven*
   See *Magnificent Seven, The.*

*Harrad Experiment, The*
1973: (Cinerama/Ted Post) James Whitmore.
1974: *Harrad Summer* (Cinerama/Steven H. Stern)
   Victoria Thompson.
*Harrad Summer*
   See *Harrad Experiment, The.*

**Going My Way. Barry Fitzgerald and Bing
Crosby.**

*Hell Up in Harlem*
   See *Black Caesar.*
*Herbie Goes to Monte Carlo*
   See *Love Bug, The.*
*Herbie Rides Again*
   See *Love Bug, The.*
*Heretic, The*
   See *Exorcist, The.*
*Horror of Dracula*
1958: (U/Terence Fisher) Christopher Lee.
1960: *Brides of Dracula, The* (U/Terence Fisher)
   Peter Cushing.
1966: *Dracula—Prince of Darkness* (Fox/Terence
   Fisher) Christopher Lee.
1968: *Dracula Has Risen From the Grave* (WB/
   Freddie Francis) Christopher Lee.
1970: *Taste the Blood of Dracula* (WB/Peter Sasdy)
   Christopher Lee.
1970: *Scars of Dracula* (Am. Cont./Roy Ward Baker)
   Christopher Lee.
1972: *Dracula A.D. 1972* (WB/Alan Gibson)
   Christopher Lee.
1973: *Satanic Rites of Dracula, The* (WB/Alan Gib-
   son) Christopher Lee.
*House of Dark Shadows*
1970: (MGM/Dan Curtis) Joan Bennett.
1971: *Night of Dark Shadows* (MGM/Dan Curtis)
   Grayson Hall.
*House of Dracula*
   See *Dracula.*
*House of Frankenstein*
   See *Dracula.*
*Huckleberry Finn*
   See *Tom Sawyer.*

*The Bells of St. Mary's.* Ingrid Bergman and
Bing Crosby.

*In Like Flint*
  See *Our Man Flint.*

*Innocents, The*
1962: (Fox/Jack Clayton) Deborah Kerr.
1972: *Nightcomers, The* (Embassy/Michael Winner)
  Marlon Brando.

*Inspector Clouseau*
  See *Pink Panther, The.*

*Interns, The*
1962: (Col/David Swift) Michael Callan.
1964: *New Interns, The* (Col/John Rich) Michael
  Callan.

*In the Heat of the Night*
1967: (UA/Norman Jewison) Sidney Poitier.
1970: *They Call Me Mister Tibbs* (UA/Gordon
  Douglas) Sidney Poitier.
1971: *Organization, The* (UA/Don Medford) Sidney
  Poitier.

*Invisible Agent*
  See *Invisible Man, The.*

*Invisible Man, The*
1933: (U/James Whale) Claude Rains.
1940: *Invisible Man Returns, The* (U/Joe May)
  Vincent Price.
1942: *Invisible Agent* (U/Edwin L. Marin) Jon Hall.
1944: *Invisible Man's Revenge, The* (U/Ford Beebe)
  Jon Hall.
1951: *Abbott and Costello Meet the Invisible Man*
  (U/Charles Lamont) Arthur Franz.

*Invisible Man Returns, The*
  See *Invisible Man, The.*

*Invisible Man's Revenge, The*
  See *Invisible Man, The.*

*Ipcress File, The*
1965: (U/Sidney J. Furie) Michael Caine.
1966: *Funeral in Berlin* (Par/Guy Hamilton) Michael
  Caine.
1967: *Billion Dollar Brain* (UA/Ken Russell) Michael
  Caine.

*Iron Mask, The*
  See *Three Musketeers, The.*

163

**The Interns. James MacArthur, Cliff Robertson, and Suzy Parker.**

**The New Interns. George Segal and Michael Callan.**

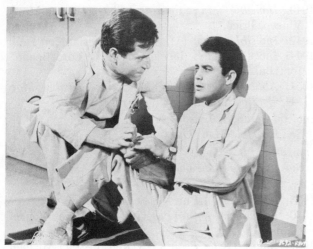

*Ivan the Terrible, Part I*
1947: (Artkino/Sergei M. Eisenstein) Nikolai Cherkassov.
1959: *Ivan the Terrible, Part II* (Janus/Sergei Eisenstein) Nikolai Cherkassov.

*Ivan the Terrible, Part II*
See *Ivan the Terrible, Part I.*

*Ivory Hunter*
1952: (U/Harry Watt) Anthony Steel.
1955: *West of Zanzibar* (Rank/Harry Watt) Anthony Steel.

*Jack Slade*
1953: (AA/Harold Schuster) Mark Stevens.
1955: *Return of Jack Slade, The* (AA/Harold Schuster) John Ericson.

*Janie*
1944: (WB/Michael Curtiz) Joyce Reynolds.
1946: *Janie Gets Married* (WB/Vincent Sherman) Joan Leslie.

*Janie Gets Married*
See *Janie.*

*Jaws*
1975: (U/Steven Spielberg) Roy Scheider.
1977: Sequel announced.

*Jesse James*
1939: (Fox/Henry King) Tyrone Power.
1940: *Return of Frank James, The* (Fox/Fritz Lang)
Henry Fonda.

*Journey Back to Oz*
See *Wizard of Oz, The.*

*King Kong*
1933: (RKO/Merian C. Cooper. Ernest B. Schoedsack) Fay Wray.
1933: *Son of Kong* (RKO/Ernest B. Schoedsack)
Robert Armstrong.

*Lady in Cement*
See *Tony Rome.*

*Lassie Come Home*
1943: (MGM/Fred M. Wilcox) Roddy McDowall.
1945: *Son of Lassie* (MGM/S. Sylvan Simon) Peter
Lawford.

*Jesse James.* **Tyrone Power, Henry Fonda,
and players. Lon Chaney, Jr., sits near
fireplace.**

*The Return of Frank James.* **Jackie Cooper,
Henry Fonda, and Gene Tierney.**

***The Maltese Falcon.* Humphrey Bogart and Elisha Cook, Jr.**

***The Black Bird.* George Segal.**

*Magnificent Seven Ride, The*
See *Magnificent Seven, The.*

*Magnum Force*
See *Dirty Harry.*

*Maltese Falcon, The*
1941: (WB/John Huston) Humphrey Bogart.
1975: *Black Bird, The* (Col/David Giler) George Segal.

*Man Called Horse, A*
1970: (NG/Elliott Silverstein) Richard Harris.
1976: *Return of a Man Called Horse, The* (UA/Irvin Kershner) Richard Harris.

*Mandingo*
1975: (Par/Richard Fleischer) James Mason.
1976: *Drum* (UA/Steve Carver) Warren Oates.

*Man With the Golden Gun, The*
See *Dr. No.*

*Mark of Zorro, The*
1920: (UA/Fred Niblo) Douglas Fairbanks.
1925: *Don Q, Son of Zorro* (UA/Donald Crisp) Douglas Fairbanks.

*Mr. Belvedere Goes to College*
See *Sitting Pretty.*

*Mr. Belvedere Rings the Bell*
See *Sitting Pretty.*

*Mister Roberts*
1955: (WB/John Ford, Mervyn LeRoy) Henry Fonda.
1964: *Ensign Pulver* (WB/Joshua Logan) Robert Walker, Jr.

*Mouse on the Moon, The*
See *Mouse that Roared, The.*

*Mouse that Roared, The*
1959: (Col/Jack Arnold) Peter Sellers.
1963: *Mouse on the Moon, The* (Lopert/Richard Lester) Margaret Rutherford.

*Mummy's Curse, The*
See *Mummy's Hand, The.*

*Mummy's Ghost, The*
See *Mummy's Hand, The.*

*Mummy's Hand, The*
1940: (U/Christy Cabanne) Tom Tyler.
1942: *Mummy's Tomb, The* (U/Harold Young) Lon Chaney, Jr.
1944: *Mummy's Ghost, The* (U/Reginald LeBorg) Lon Chaney, Jr.
1945: *Mummy's Curse, The* (U/Leslie Goodwin) Lon Chaney, Jr.
1955: *Abbott and Costello Meet the Mummy* (U/Charles Lamont) Michael Ansara.

*Mummy's Tomb, The*
See *Mummy's Hand, The.*

*Murderers' Row*
See *Silencers, The.*

*My Friend Flicka*
1943: (Fox/Harold Schuster) Preston Foster.
1945: *Thunderhead—Son of Flicka* (Fox/Louis King) Preston Foster.

*My Friend Irma*
1949: (Par/George Marshall) Marie Wilson.
1950: *My Friend Irma Goes West* (Par/Hal Walker) Marie Wilson.

*My Friend Irma Goes West*
See *My Friend Irma.*

*McHale's Navy*
1964: (U/Edward J. Montagne) Ernest Borgnine.
1965: *McHale's Navy Joins the Air Force* (U/Edward J. Montagne) Joe Flynn.

*McHale's Navy Joins the Air Force*
See *McHale's Navy.*

*New Interns, The*
See *Interns, The.*

*New Land, The*
See *Emigrants, The.*

*Nightcomers, The*
See *Innocents, The.*

*Night of Dark Shadows*
See *House of Dark Shadows.*

*Now You See Him, Now You Don't*
See *Computer Wore Tennis Shoes, The.*

*Oh, Alfie!*
See *Alfie!*

*The Mouse that Roared.* Peter Sellers.

*The Mouse on the Moon.* Ron Moody and Margaret Rutherford.

168

*Omen, The*
1976: (Fox/Richard Donner) Gregory Peck.
1977: Sequel announced.
*One More Time*
See *Salt and Pepper.*
*On Her Majesty's Secret Service*
See *Dr. No.*
*On Moonlight Bay*
1951: (WB/Roy Del Ruth) Doris Day.
1953: *By the Light of the Silvery Moon* (WB/David Butler) Doris Day.
*Organization, The*
See *In the Heat of the Night.*
*Other Side of the Mountain, The*
1975: (U/Larry Peerce) Marilyn Hassett.
1977: Sequel announced.
*Our Hearts Were Growing Up*
See *Our Hearts Were Young and Gay.*
*Our Hearts Were Young and Gay*
1944: (Par/Lewis Allen) Gail Russell.
1946: *Our Hearts Were Growing Up* (Par/William D. Russell) Gail Russell.
*Our Man Flint*
1966: (Fox/Daniel Mann) James Coburn.
1967: *In Like Flint* (Fox/Gordon Douglas) James Coburn.

*Part II, Sounder*
See *Sounder.*
*Part II, Walking Tall*
See *Walking Tall.*
*Paul and Michelle*
See *Friends.*
*Percy*
1971: (MGM/Ralph Thomas) Hywel Bennett.
1975: *Percy's Progress* (MGM/Ralph Thomas) Leigh Lawson.
*Percy's Progress*
See *Percy.*
*Pink Panther, The*
1964: (UA/Blake Edwards) David Niven.
1964: *Shot in the Dark, A* (UA/Blake Edwards) Peter Sellers.
1968: *Inspector Clouseau* (UA/Bud Yorkin) Alan Arkin.
1975: *Return of the Pink Panther, The* (UA/Blake Edwards) Peter Sellers.
1976: *Pink Panther Strikes Again, The* (UA/Blake Edwards) Peter Sellers.
*Pink Panther Strikes Again, The*
See *Pink Panther, The.*
*Poseidon Adventure, The*
1972: (Fox/Ronald Neame) Gene Hackman.
1977: Sequel announced.
*Pure Hell of St. Trinian's, The*
See *Belles of St. Trinian's, The*

**On Moonlight Bay. Doris Day, Gordon MacRae, and player.**

**By the Light of the Silvery Moon. Rosemary DeCamp, Gordon MacRae, Doris Day, Leon Ames, and Mary Wickes.**

*Red Stallion, The*
1947: (EL/Lesley Selander) Robert Paige.
1949: *Red Stallion in the Rockies* (EL/Ralph Murphy) Arthur Franz.
*Red Stallion in the Rockies*
See *Red Stallion, The.*
*Return of a Man Called Horse, The*
See *Man Called Horse, A.*
*Return of Count Yorga*
See *Court Yorga, Vampire.*
*Return of Frank James, The*
See *Jesse James.*
*Return of Jack Slade, The*
See *Jack Slade.*
*Return of the Fly, The*
See *Fly, The.*

*Return of the Pink Panther, The*
  See *Pink Panther, The.*
*Return of the Scarlet Pimpernel, The*
  See *Scarlet Pimpernel, The.*
*Return of the Seven*
  See *Magnificent Seven, The.*
*Return to Macon County*
  See *Macon County Line.*
*Rooster Cogburn*
  See *True Grit.*

*Salt and Pepper*
1968: (UA/Richard Donner) Sammy Davis, Jr.
1970: *One More Time* (UA/Jerry Lewis) Sammy Davis, Jr.
*Satanic Rites of Dracula, The*
  See *Horror of Dracula.*
*Scarlet Pimpernel, The*
1935: (UA/Harold Young) Leslie Howard.
1938: *Return of the Scarlet Pimpernel, The* (UA/Hans Schwartz) Barry Barnes.
*Scars of Dracula*
  See *Horror of Dracula.*
*Scream Blacula Scream*
  See *Blacula.*
*See Here, Private Hargrove*
1944: (MGM/Wesley Ruggles) Robert Walker.
1945: *What Next, Corporal Hargrove?* (MGM/Richard Thorpe) Robert Walker.
*Shaft*
1971: (MGM/Gordon Parks) Richard Roundtree.
1972: *Shaft's Big Score* (MGM/Gordon Parks) Richard Roundtree.
1973: *Shaft in Africa* (MGM/John Guillermin) Richard Roundtree.
*Shaft in Africa*
  See *Shaft.*
*Shaft's Big Score*
  See *Shaft.*
*She*
1965: (MGM/Robert Day) Ursula Andress.
1968: *Vengeance of She, The* (Fox/Cliff Owen) John Richardson.
*Sheik, The*
1921: (Par/George Melford) Rudolph Valentino.
1926: *Son of the Sheik, The* (UA/George Fitzmaurice) Rudolph Valentino.
*Shot in the Dark, A*
  See *Pink Panther, The.*
*Silencers, The*
1966: (Col/Phil Karlson) Dean Martin.
1966: *Murderers' Row* (Col/Henry Levin) Dean Martin.

**See Here, Private Hargrove. Douglas Fowle Robert Walker, and Donald Curtis.**

**What Next, Corporal Hargrove?. Robert Walker and Chill Wills.**

1967: *Ambushers, The* (Col/Henry Levin) Dean Martin.
1968: *Wrecking Crew, The* (Col/Phil Karlson) Dean Martin.
*Sitting Pretty*
1948: Fox/Walter Lang) Clifton Webb.
1949: *Mr. Belvedere Goes to College* (Fox/Eliott Nugent) Clifton Webb.
1951: *Mr. Belvedere Rings the Bell* (Fox/Henry Koster) Clifton Webb.
*Slaughter*
1972: (AIP/Jack Starrett) Jim Brown.
1973: *Slaughter's Big Rip-Off* (AIP/Gordon Douglas) Jim Brown.
*Slaughter's Big Rip-Off*
  See *Slaughter.*
*Son of Blob*
  See *Blob, The.*
*Son of Captain Blood, The*
  See *Captain Blood.*
*Son of Dracula*
  See *Dracula.*
*Son of Flubber*
  See *Absent-Minded Professor, The.*
*Son of Frankenstein*
  See *Dracula.*
*Son of Kong*
  See *King Kong.*
*Son of Lassie*
  See *Lassie Come Home.*

**Son of the Sheik, The**
  See *Sheik, The.*

**Sounder**
1972: (Fox/Martin Ritt) Cicely Tyson.
1976: *Part II, Sounder* (Gamma III/William Graham)
  Ebony Wright.

**Spy Who Loved Me, The**
  See *Dr. No.*

**Sting, The**
1973: (U/George Roy Hill) Paul Newman.
1977: Sequel announced.

**Strongest Man in the World, The**
  See *Computer Wore Tennis Shoes, The.*

**Summer of '42**
1971: (WB/Richard Mulligan) Gary Grimes.
1973: *Class of '44* (WB/Paul Bogart) Gary Grimes.

**Tammy and the Bachelor**
1957: (U/Joseph Pevney) Debbie Reynolds.
1961: *Tammy Tell Me True* (U/Harry Keller) Sandra
  Dee.

1963: *Tammy and the Doctor* (U/Harry Keller)
  Sandra Dee.

**Tammy and the Doctor**
  See *Tammy and the Bachelor.*

**Tammy Tell Me True**
  See *Tammy and the Bachelor.*

**Taste the Blood of Dracula**
  See *Horror of Dracula.*

**That's Entertainment!**
1974: (MGM/Jack Haley, Jr.) Gene Kelly.
1976: *That's Entertainment,* Part II (MGM/Gene
  Kelly) Fred Astaire.

**That' Entertainment, Part II**
  See *That's Entertainment!*

**They Call Me Mister Tibbs**
  See *In the Heat of the Night.*

**Three Musketeers, The**
1921: (UA/Fred Niblo) Douglas Fairbanks.
1929: *Iron Mask, The* (UA/Allan Dwan) Douglas
  Fairbanks.

*True Grit.* John Wayne.

*Rooster Cogburn.* John Wayne and Katharine Hepburn.

*Three Smart Girls*
1937: (U/Henry Koster) Binnie Barnes.
1939: *Three Smart Girls Grow Up* (U/Henry Koster)
Deanna Durbin.

*Three Smart Girls Grow Up*
See *Three Smart Girls*.

*Thunderball*
See *Dr. No*.

*Thunderhead—Son of Flicka*
See *My Friend Flicka*.

*Tom Sawyer*
1973: (UA/Don Taylor) Johnny Whitaker.
1974: *Huckleberry Finn* (UA/J. Lee Thompson) Jeff East.

*Tony Rome*
1967: (Fox/Gordon Douglas) Frank Sinatra.
1968: *Lady in Cement* (Fox/Gordon Douglas) Frank Sinatra.

*Treasure Island*
1950: (Disney/Byron Haskin) Robert Newton.
1954: *Long John Silver* (NET/Byron Haskin) Robert Newton.

*Trial of Billy Jack, The*
See *Born Losers*.

*Trouble With Angels, The*
1966: (Col/Ida Lupino) Rosalind Russell.
1968: *Where Angels Go . . . Trouble Follows* (Col/James Neilson) Rosalind Russell.

*True Grit*
1969: (Par/Henry Hathaway) John Wayne.
1975: *Rooster Cogburn* (U/Stuart Millar) John Wayne.

*Up From the Beach*
See *Longest Day. The.*

*Up Front*
1951: (U/Alexander Knox) David Wayne.
1952: *Willie and Joe Back at the Front* (U/George Sherman) Tom Ewell.

*Vengeance of She, The*
See *She.*

*Village of the Damned*
1960: (MGM/Wolf Rilla) George Sanders.
1964: *Children of the Damned* (MGM/Antone Leader) Ian Hendry.

*Walking Tall*
1973: (Cinerama/Phil Karlson) Joe Don Baker.
1975: *Part II, Walking Tall* (Cinerama/Earl Bellamy) Bo Svenson.
1977: *Final Chapter—Walking Tall* (AIP/Jack Starrett) Bo Svenson.

*West of Zanzibar*
See *Ivory Hunter.*

*What Price Glory.* Victor McLaglen, Dolores Del Rio, and Edmund Lowe.

*Westworld*
1973: (MGM/Michael Crichton) Yul Brynner.
1976: *Futureworld* (AIP/Richard Heffron) Peter Fonda.

*What Next, Corporal Hargrove?*
See *See Here, Private Hargrove.*

*What Price Glory*
1926: (Fox/Raoul Walsh) Edmund Lowe.
1929: *Cockeyed World, The* (Fox/Raoul Walsh) Edmund Lowe.
1931: *Women of All Nations* (Fox/Raoul Walsh) Edmund Lowe.

*Where Angels Go . . . Trouble Follows*
See *Trouble With Angels, The.*

*Whistling in Brooklyn*
See *Whistling in the Dark.*

*Whistling in Dixie*
See *Whistling in the Dark.*

*Whistling in the Dark*
1941: (MGM/S. Sylvan Simon) Red Skelton.
1942: *Whistling in Dixie* (MGM/S. Sylvan Simon) Red Skelton.
1943: *Whistling in Brooklyn* (MGM/S. Sylvan Simon) Red Skelton.

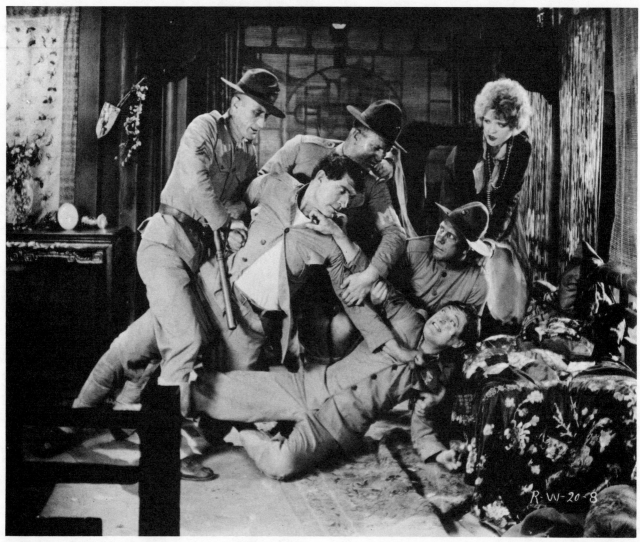

*The Cockeyed World.* Victor McLaglen, Edmund Lowe, and players.

*Women of All Nations.* Humphrey Bogart, Edmund Lowe, Victor McLaglen, and player.

*Young Tom Edison.* Harry Shannon and Mickey Rooney.

*White Lightning*
1973: (UA/Joseph Sargent) Burt Reynolds.
1976: *Gator* (UA/Burt Reynolds) Burt Reynolds.
*Willard*
1971: (Cinerama/Daniel Mann) Bruce Davison.
1972: *Ben* (Cinerama/Phil Karlson) Joseph Campanella.
*Willie and Joe Back at the Front*
    See *Up Front.*
*Wizard of Oz, The*
1939: (MGM/Victor Fleming) Judy Garland.
1974: *Journey Back to Oz* (Filmation/Animation) Liza Minnelli.
*Wolf Man, The*
    See *Dracula.*

*Women of All Nations*
    See *What Price Glory.*
*Wrecking Crew, The*
    See *Silencers, The.*

*Younger Brothers, The*
    See *Bad Men of Missouri.*
*Young Tom Edison*
1940: (MGM/Norman Taurog) Mickey Rooney.
1940: *Edison, the Man* (MGM/Clarence Brown) Spencer Tracy.
*You Only Live Twice*
    See *Dr. No.*

**Edison, *the* Man. Rita Johnson, Spencer Tracy, Henry Travers, and players.**

175